Presented to

Our Deb

By

Tom & Jeanine
Christmas 2001

GOD'S PROMISES

— & —

ANSWERS

FOR YOUR LIFE

COUNTRYMAN
®

A Division of Thomas Nelson
Nashville

God's Promises for Your Every Need—originally compiled by Dr. A. L. Gill

God's Answers for Your Life—originally compiled by Kay Wheeler Kilgore

Both original compilations have been modified and edited by the J. Countryman Editorial Staff for this edition

Cover design by David Uttley, David Uttley Design, Sisters, Oregon

ISBN: 0-8499-5581-5

Printed in Mexico

CONTENTS

GOD'S PROMISES
FOR YOUR EVERY NEED

JESUS IS YOUR . . .

Savior	2
Lord	5
Love	8
Peace	11
Forgiveness	13
Righteousness	16
Deliverer	19
Fellowship	21
Example	24
Companion	27
Brother	29
Guardian	31
Security	34
Sufficiency	37
Fulfillment	40
Everything	43

THE BIBLE IS YOUR . . .

Infallible Authority	46
Deed of Inheritance	49
Guide for Life	52

Contents

Stability   55
Strength   57

WHAT TO DO WHEN YOU FEEL . . .
Discouraged   61
Worried   63
Lonely   66
Depressed   69
Dissatisfied   71
Condemned   74
Confused   77
Tempted   79
Angry   82
Rebellious   85

WHAT TO DO WHEN YOU ARE . . .
Experiencing Fear   88
Emotionally Distraught   91
In Need of Courage   93
In Need of Patience   96
In Need of Peace   99
Lukewarm Spiritually   102
Grieving   105
Doubting God   108

WHAT TO DO WHEN . . .
You Need Confidence   112
You Have Troubles in Your Life   115
You Have Financial Troubles   118

Contents

You Have Marital Problems 121
You Are Deserted by Loved Ones 124
You Don't Understand God's Ways 127
You Are Waiting on God 130

WHAT THE BIBLE HAS TO SAY ABOUT . . .

Faith 133
Love 136
Eternity 139
Praise 142
Serving God 145
Obedience 148
The Carnal Mind 151
The Grace of God 154
The Holy Spirit 157
God's Faithfulness 160
The Church 163
Stewardship 166
Satan 169
The Return of Christ 172
The Unsaved 175

TRUTH FROM THE BIBLE ABOUT . . .

Forgiving Others 179
Christian Fellowship 182
Your Responsibility 185
Speaking God's Word 188
Finding the Will of God 191

Contents

Answered Prayer   194
Unsaved Loved Ones   197
Marriage   199
Divorce   202
Your Family   205
Wives   208
Widows   211
Singles   214
The Elderly   217

WHAT YOU CAN DO TO . . .
Grow Spiritually   221
Change the World   224
Help Your Business   227
Please God   230

GOD'S PLAN OF SALVATION   234

GOD'S ANSWERS
FOR YOUR LIFE

BEGINNING IN CHRIST
How to Know You Are Born Again   240
How to Know the Sufficiency of Jesus   243
What the Blood of Jesus Is to You   246
How to Know the Power of God's Word   249
What the Holy Spirit Is to You   252
How to Abide in Christ   255

How to Build Your Faith 258

GROWING IN CHRIST

How to Overcome the Carnal Mind 262
How to Overcome Satan 265
How to Recognize Evil 268
How to Overcome Worldliness 271
How to Deal with Lust 274
How to Overcome Pride 277
How to Control Your Tongue 280
How to Be Christ-Centered 283
Understanding the Liberty that Is in Christ 286
How to Praise the Lord 289
How to Have the Joy of the Lord 292

MATURING IN CHRIST

How to Handle Spiritual Trials 296
How to Face Serious Illness 299
How to Handle Suffering 302
How to Survive Financial Problems 305
How to Handle Stress 308
How to Overcome Despair 312
How to Maintain Hope 315
How to Enter Into God's Rest 318
How to Be Established in Trust 320
How to Face Old Age 323
How to Have God's Divine Protection 326
How to Find Contentment 329

Contents

MINISTERING IN CHRIST

What Is True Service? 333
How to Have an Effective Prayer Life 336
How to Be an Effective Witness 339
How to Handle Condemnation 342
Understanding the Leading of the Lord 345
How to Wait on God 348
The Importance of Obedience 351
Giving to God's Work 354

HOPING IN CHRIST

How to Commit Your Life to Christ 358
How to Draw Near to God 361
How to Recover Spiritually 364
How to Obtain God's Promises 367

UNDERSTANDING IN CHRIST

Understanding the Personality of God 372
How to Receive Understanding 375
Understanding the Fear of the Lord 378
Understanding the Sovereignty of God 381
How to Grasp Eternity 384

UNITING IN CHRIST

The Fellowship of All Believers 388
The Hope for Revival 391
The Signs of the End 394

GOD'S PROMISES

For Your Every Need

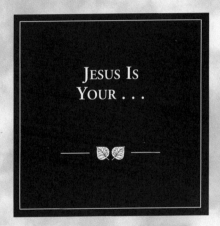

JESUS IS
YOUR . . .

Jesus Is Your Savior

Not by works of righteousness which we have done, but according to His mercy He saved us, through the washing of regeneration and renewing of the Holy Spirit, whom He poured out on us abundantly through Jesus Christ our Savior.

Titus 3:5, 6

We have seen and testify that the Father has sent the Son as Savior of the world.

1 John 4:14

My spirit has rejoiced in God my Savior.

Luke 1:47

We ourselves have heard Him and we know that this is indeed the Christ, the Savior of the world.

John 4:42b

The Son of Man has come to seek and to save that which was lost.

Luke 19:10

For God so loved the world that He gave His only begotten Son, that whoever believes in Him should not perish but have everlasting life.

JOHN 3:16

Being justified freely by His grace through the redemption that is in Christ Jesus, whom God set forth as a propitiation by His blood, through faith, to demonstrate His righteousness, because in His forbearance God had passed over the sins that were previously committed.

ROMANS 3:24, 25

But God, who is rich in mercy, because of His great love with which He loved us, even when we were dead in trespasses, made us alive together with Christ (by grace you have been saved).

EPHESIANS 2:4, 5

Most assuredly, I say to you, he who believes in Me has everlasting life.

JOHN 6:47

For by grace you have been saved through faith, and that not of yourselves; it is the gift of God, not of works, lest anyone should boast.

EPHESIANS 2:8, 9

If you confess with your mouth the Lord Jesus and believe in your heart that God has raised Him from the dead, you will be saved.

ROMANS 10:9

If anyone is in Christ, he is a new creation; old things have passed away; behold, all things have become new.

2 CORINTHIANS 5:17

Who has saved us and called us with a holy calling, not according to our works, but according to His own purpose and grace which was given to us in Christ Jesus before time began.

2 TIMOTHY 1:9

Nevertheless He saved them for His name's sake, that He might make His mighty power known.

PSALM 106:8

JESUS IS YOUR LORD

Therefore God also has highly exalted Him and given Him the name which is above every name, that at the name of Jesus every knee should bow, of those in heaven, and of those on earth, and of those under the earth, and that every tongue should confess that Jesus Christ is Lord, to the glory of God the Father.

PHILIPPIANS 2:9–11

Why do you call Me "Lord, Lord," and not do the things which I say?

LUKE 6:46

I beseech you therefore, brethren, by the mercies of God, that you present your bodies a living sacrifice, holy, acceptable to God, which is your reasonable service.

And do not be conformed to this world, but be transformed by the renewing of your mind, that you may prove what is that good and acceptable and perfect will of God.

ROMANS 12:1, 2

For sin shall not have dominion over you, for you are not under law but under grace.

What then? Shall we sin because we are not under law but under grace? Certainly not!

Do you not know that to whom you present yourselves slaves to obey, you are that one's slaves whom you obey, whether of sin leading to death, or of obedience leading to righteousness?

ROMANS 6:14–16

Do you not know that your body is the temple of the Holy Spirit who is in you, whom you have from God, and you are not your own?

For you were bought at a price; therefore glorify God in your body and in your spirit, which are God's.

1 CORINTHIANS 6:19, 20

Let all the house of Israel know assuredly that God has made this Jesus, whom you crucified, both Lord and Christ.

ACTS 2:36

If we live, we live to the Lord; and if we die, we die to the Lord. Therefore, whether we live or die, we are the Lord's.

ROMANS 14:8

> For the Lord GOD will help Me;
> Therefore I will not be disgraced;
> Therefore I have set My face like a flint,
> And I know that I will not be ashamed.

ISAIAH 50:7

"You shall love the LORD your God with all your heart, with all your soul, with all your mind, and with all your strength." This is the first commandment.

MARK 12:30

JESUS IS YOUR LOVE

The LORD will command His lovingkindness in the
  daytime,
And in the night His song shall be with me—
A prayer to the God of my life.

PSALM 42:8

Beloved, let us love one another, for love is of God; and
everyone who loves is born of God and knows God.

He who does not love does not know God, for God
is love.

In this the love of God was manifested toward us,
that God has sent His only begotten Son into the
world, that we might live through Him.

In this is love, not that we loved God, but that He
loved us and sent His Son to be the propitiation for
our sins.

Beloved, if God so loved us, we also ought to love
one another.

No one has seen God at any time. If we love one
another, God abides in us, and His love has been perfected in us.

1 JOHN 4:7–12

And we have known and believed the love that God has for us. God is love, and he who abides in love abides in God, and God in him.

We love Him because He first loved us.

1 JOHN 4:16, 19

As the Father loved Me, I also have loved you; abide in My love.

If you keep My commandments, you will abide in My love, just as I have kept My Father's commandments and abide in His love.

These things I have spoken to you, that My joy may remain in you, and that your joy may be full.

This is My commandment, that you love one another as I have loved you.

Greater love has no one than this, than to lay down one's life for his friends.

These things I command you, that you love one another.

JOHN 15:9–13, 17

He who has My commandments and keeps them, it is he who loves Me. And he who loves Me will be loved by My Father, and I will love him and manifest Myself to him.

JOHN 14:21

But God demonstrates His own love toward us, in that while we were still sinners, Christ died for us.

ROMANS 5:8

That Christ may dwell in your hearts through faith; that you, being rooted and grounded in love, may be able to comprehend with all the saints what is the width and length and depth and height—to know the love of Christ which passes knowledge; that you may be filled with all the fullness of God.

EPHESIANS 3:17–19

I love those who love me, and those who seek me diligently will find me.

PROVERBS 8:17

The LORD has appeared of old to me, saying:
"Yes, I have loved you with an everlasting love;
Therefore with lovingkindness I have drawn you."

JEREMIAH 31:3

I will betroth you to Me forever;
Yes, I will betroth you to Me
In righteousness and justice,
In lovingkindness and mercy.

HOSEA 2:19

Jesus Is Your Peace

You will keep him in perfect peace, whose mind is stayed on You, because he trusts in You.

ISAIAH 26:3

But now in Christ Jesus you who once were far off have been brought near by the blood of Christ.

For He Himself is our peace, who has made both one, and has broken down the middle wall of separation.

EPHESIANS 2:13, 14

The God of peace will crush Satan under your feet shortly. The grace of our Lord Jesus Christ be with you.

ROMANS 16:20

The things which you learned and received and heard and saw in me, these do, and the God of peace will be with you.

PHILIPPIANS 4:9

And let the peace of God rule in your hearts, to which also you were called in one body; and be thankful.

COLOSSIANS 3:15

The LORD will give strength to His people;
The LORD will bless His people with peace.

PSALM 29:11

Peace I leave with you, My peace I give to you; not as the world gives do I give to you. Let not your heart be troubled, neither let it be afraid.

JOHN 14:27

Jesus Is Your Forgiveness

To the praise of the glory of His grace, by which He made us accepted in the Beloved.

In Him we have redemption through His blood, the forgiveness of sins, according to the riches of His grace.

Ephesians 1:6, 7

You have forgiven the iniquity of Your people;
You have covered all their sin.

Psalm 85:2

As far as the east is from the west,
So far has He removed our transgressions from us.

Psalm 103:12

My little children, these things I write to you, so that you may not sin. And if anyone sins, we have an Advocate with the Father, Jesus Christ the righteous.

1 John 2:1

If we confess our sins, He is faithful and just to forgive us our sins and to cleanse us from all unrighteousness.

1 JOHN 1:9

I will be merciful to their unrighteousness, and their sins and their lawless deeds I will remember no more.

HEBREWS 8:12

> Let the wicked forsake his way,
> And the unrighteous man his thoughts;
> Let him return to the LORD,
> And He will have mercy on him;
> And to our God,
> For He will abundantly pardon.

ISAIAH 55:7

You, being dead in your trespasses and the uncircumcision of your flesh, He has made alive together with Him, having forgiven you all trespasses.

COLOSSIANS 2:13

I will cleanse them from all their iniquity by which they have sinned against Me, and I will pardon all their iniquities by which they have sinned and by which they have transgressed against Me.

JEREMIAH 33:8

"Come now, and let us reason together,"
  Says the LORD,
"Though your sins are like scarlet,
  They shall be as white as snow;
  Though they are red like crimson,
  They shall be as wool."

ISAIAH 1:18

I, even I, am He who blots out your transgressions for My own sake; and I will not remember your sins.

ISAIAH 43:25

Blessed is he whose transgression is forgiven, whose sin is covered.

Blessed is the man to whom the LORD does not impute iniquity, and in whose spirit there is no deceit.

PSALM 32:1, 2

JESUS IS YOUR RIGHTEOUSNESS

He made Him who knew no sin to be sin for us, that we might become the righteousness of God in Him.

2 CORINTHIANS 5:21

Of Him you are in Christ Jesus, who became for us wisdom from God—and righteousness and sanctification and redemption.

1 CORINTHIANS 1:30

[Being] found in Him, not having my own righteousness, which is from the law, but that which is through faith in Christ, the righteousness which is from God by faith.

PHILIPPIANS 3:9

Just as Abraham "believed God, and it was accounted to him for righteousness." Therefore know that only those who are of faith are sons of Abraham.

GALATIANS 3:6, 7

To him who does not work but believes on Him who justifies the ungodly, his faith is accounted for righteousness.

ROMANS 4:5

If by the one man's offense death reigned through the one, much more those who receive abundance of grace and of the gift of righteousness will reign in life through the One, Jesus Christ.

ROMANS 5:17

What the law could not do in that it was weak through the flesh, God did by sending His own Son in the likeness of sinful flesh, on account of sin: He condemned sin in the flesh, that the righteous require-ment of the law might be fulfilled in us who do not walk according to the flesh but according to the Spirit.

ROMANS 8:3, 4

What shall we say then? That Gentiles, who did not pursue righteousness, have attained to righteousness, even the righteousness of faith.

ROMANS 9:30

Whom He foreknew, He also predestined to be conformed to the image of His Son, that He might be the firstborn among many brethren.

Moreover whom He predestined, these He also called; whom He called, these He also justified; and whom He justified, these He also glorified.

ROMANS 8:29, 30

The work of righteousness will be peace, and the effect of righteousness, quietness and assurance forever.

ISAIAH 32:17

With the heart one believes unto righteousness, and with the mouth confession is made unto salvation.

ROMANS 10:10

JESUS IS YOUR DELIVERER

The Spirit of the Lord GOD is upon Me,
Because the LORD has anointed Me
To preach good tidings to the poor;
He has sent Me to heal the brokenhearted,
To proclaim liberty to the captives,
And the opening of the prison to those who are
  bound.

ISAIAH 61:1

You shall know the truth, and the truth shall make
you free.

Therefore if the Son makes you free, you shall be
free indeed.

JOHN 8:32, 36

The law of the Spirit of life in Christ Jesus has made
me free from the law of sin and death.

ROMANS 8:2

These signs will follow those who believe: In My
name they will cast out demons; they will speak with
new tongues.

MARK 16:17

You have broken the yoke of his burden and the staff of his shoulder, the rod of his oppressor, as in the day of Midian.

Isaiah 9:4

> The Spirit of the LORD is upon Me,
> Because He has anointed Me
> To preach the gospel to the poor;
> He has sent Me to heal the brokenhearted,
> To proclaim liberty to the captives
> And recovery of sight to the blind,
> To set at liberty those who are oppressed.

Luke 4:18

Behold, I give you the authority to trample on serpents and scorpions, and over all the power of the enemy, and nothing shall by any means hurt you.

Luke 10:19

Having been set free from sin, and having become slaves of God, you have your fruit to holiness, and the end, everlasting life.

Romans 6:22

Jesus Is Your Fellowship

That which we have seen and heard we declare to you, that you also may have fellowship with us; and truly our fellowship is with the Father and with His Son Jesus Christ.

1 John 1:3

God is faithful, by whom you were called into the fellowship of His Son, Jesus Christ our Lord.

1 Corinthians 1:9

Behold, I stand at the door and knock. If anyone hears My voice and opens the door, I will come in to him and dine with him, and he with Me.

Revelation 3:20

Jesus answered and said to him, "If anyone loves Me, he will keep My word; and My Father will love him, and We will come to him and make Our home with him."

John 14:23

"Sing and rejoice, O daughter of Zion! For behold, I am coming and I will dwell in your midst," says the LORD.

ZECHARIAH 2:10

For where two or three are gathered together in My name, I am there in the midst of them.

MATTHEW 18:20

Abide in Me, and I in you. As the branch cannot bear fruit of itself, unless it abides in the vine, neither can you, unless you abide in Me.

I am the vine, you are the branches. He who abides in Me, and I in him, bears much fruit; for without Me you can do nothing.

If you abide in Me, and My words abide in you, you will ask what you desire, and it shall be done for you.

JOHN 15:4, 5, 7

Therefore if there is any consolation in Christ, if any comfort of love, if any fellowship of the Spirit, if any affection and mercy, fulfill my joy by being like-minded, having the same love, being of one accord, of one mind.

PHILIPPIANS 2:1, 2

I am a companion of all who fear You, and of those who keep Your precepts.

PSALM 119:63

Walk in love, as Christ also has loved us and given Himself for us, an offering and a sacrifice to God for a sweet-smelling aroma.

Speaking to one another in psalms and hymns and spiritual songs, singing and making melody in your heart to the Lord. . . .

For we are members of His body, of His flesh and of His bones.

EPHESIANS 5:2, 19, 30

This is the message which we have heard from Him and declare to you, that God is light and in Him is no darkness at all.

If we say that we have fellowship with Him, and walk in darkness, we lie and do not practice the truth.

But if we walk in the light as He is in the light, we have fellowship with one another, and the blood of Jesus Christ His Son cleanses us from all sin.

1 JOHN 1:5–7

Jesus Is Your Example

To this you were called, because Christ also suffered for us, leaving us an example, that you should follow His steps.

1 Peter 2:21

He who says he abides in Him ought himself also to walk just as He walked.

1 John 2:6

If I then, your Lord and Teacher, have washed your feet, you also ought to wash one another's feet.

For I have given you an example, that you should do as I have done to you.

John 13:14, 15

Let this mind be in you which was also in Christ Jesus, who, being in the form of God, did not consider it robbery to be equal with God, but made Himself of no reputation, taking the form of a bondservant, and coming in the likeness of men.

And being found in appearance as a man, He humbled Himself and became obedient to the point of death, even the death of the cross.

PHILIPPIANS 2:5–8

Whoever desires to become great among you shall be your servant.

And whoever of you desires to be first shall be slave of all.

For even the Son of Man did not come to be served, but to serve, and to give His life a ransom for many.

MARK 10:43–45

A new commandment I give to you, that you love one another; as I have loved you, that you also love one another.

JOHN 13:34

By this we know love, because He laid down His life for us. And we also ought to lay down our lives for the brethren.

1 JOHN 3:16

Now may the God of patience and comfort grant you to be like-minded toward one another, according to Christ Jesus, that you may with one mind and one mouth glorify the God and Father of our Lord Jesus Christ.

Therefore receive one another, just as Christ also received us, to the glory of God.

ROMANS 15:5–7

Looking unto Jesus, the author and finisher of our faith, who for the joy that was set before Him endured the cross, despising the shame, and has sat down at the right hand of the throne of God.

For consider Him who endured such hostility from sinners against Himself, lest you become weary and discouraged in your souls.

HEBREWS 12:2, 3

JESUS IS YOUR COMPANION

A man who has friends must himself be friendly, but there is a friend who sticks closer than a brother.

PROVERBS 18:24

Let your conduct be without covetousness; be content with such things as you have. For He Himself has said, "I will never leave you nor forsake you."

HEBREWS 13:5

No longer do I call you servants, for a servant does not know what his master is doing; but I have called you friends, for all things that I heard from My Father I have made known to you.

You did not choose Me, but I chose you and appointed you that you should go and bear fruit, and that your fruit should remain, that whatever you ask the Father in My name He may give you.

JOHN 15:15, 16

Draw near to God and He will draw near to you. Cleanse your hands, you sinners; and purify your hearts, you double-minded.

JAMES 4:8

"For the mountains shall depart
And the hills be removed,
But My kindness shall not depart from you,
Nor shall My covenant of peace be removed,"
Says the LORD, who has mercy on you.

ISAIAH 54:10

When my father and my mother forsake me,
Then the LORD will take care of me.

PSALM 27:10

You are My friends if you do whatever I command you.

JOHN 15:14

I will not leave you orphans; I will come to you.

JOHN 14:18

Jesus is Your Brother

For whoever does the will of My Father in heaven is My brother and sister and mother.

MATTHEW 12:50

Both He who sanctifies and those who are being sanctified are all of one, for which reason He is not ashamed to call them brethren.

HEBREWS 2:11

For you are all sons of God through faith in Christ Jesus.

GALATIANS 3:26

As many as received Him, to them He gave the right to become children of God, to those who believe in His name.

JOHN 1:12

Behold what manner of love the Father has bestowed on us, that we should be called children of God! Therefore the world does not know us, because it did not know Him.

1 JOHN 3:1

Because you are sons, God has sent forth the Spirit of His Son into your hearts, crying out, "Abba, Father!"

Therefore you are no longer a slave but a son, and if a son, then an heir of God through Christ.

GALATIANS 4:6, 7

For as many as are led by the Spirit of God, these are sons of God.

ROMANS 8:14

Beloved, now we are children of God; and it has not yet been revealed what we shall be, but we know that when He is revealed, we shall be like Him, for we shall see Him as He is.

1 JOHN 3:2

Jesus Is Your Guardian

When you pass through the waters, I will be with you; and through the rivers, they shall not overflow you. When you walk through the fire, you shall not be burned, nor shall the flame scorch you.

ISAIAH 43:2

But You, O LORD, are a shield for me, my glory and the One who lifts up my head.

PSALM 3:3

The eyes of the LORD run to and fro throughout the whole earth, to show Himself strong on behalf of those whose heart is loyal to Him.

2 CHRONICLES 16:9a

The LORD your God, who goes before you, He will fight for you, according to all He did for you in Egypt before your eyes.

DEUTERONOMY 1:30

But the Lord is faithful, who will establish you and guard you from the evil one.

2 THESSALONIANS 3:3

If you indeed obey His voice and do all that I speak, then I will be an enemy to your enemies and an adversary to your adversaries.

EXODUS 23:22

He will guard the feet of His saints, but the wicked shall be silent in darkness. For by strength no man shall prevail.

1 SAMUEL 2:9

You have been a shelter for me, a strong tower from the enemy.

PSALM 61:3

The LORD your God in your midst,
The Mighty One, will save;
He will rejoice over you with gladness,
He will quiet you with His love,
He will rejoice over you with singing.

ZEPHANIAH 3:17

A thousand may fall at your side, and ten thousand at your right hand; but it shall not come near you.

PSALM 91:7

The eyes of the LORD are on the righteous, and His ears are open to their prayers; but the face of the LORD is against those who do evil.

And who is he who will harm you if you become followers of what is good?

1 PETER 3:12, 13

The eternal God is your refuge, and underneath are the everlasting arms; He will thrust out the enemy from before you, and will say, "Destroy!"

DEUTERONOMY 33:27

So shall they fear the name of the LORD from the west, and His glory from the rising of the sun; when the enemy comes in like a flood, the Spirit of the LORD will lift up a standard against him.

ISAIAH 59:19

JESUS IS YOUR SECURITY

Blessed be the God and Father of our Lord Jesus Christ, who according to His abundant mercy has begotten us again to a living hope through the resurrection of Jesus Christ from the dead, to an inheritance incorruptible and undefiled and that does not fade away, reserved in heaven for you, who are kept by the power of God through faith for salvation ready to be revealed in the last time.

1 PETER 1:3–5

My sheep hear My voice, and I know them, and they follow Me.

And I give them eternal life, and they shall never perish; neither shall anyone snatch them out of My hand.

My Father, who has given them to Me, is greater than all; and no one is able to snatch them out of My Father's hand.

JOHN 10:27–29

Who also has sealed us and given us the Spirit in our hearts as a guarantee.

2 CORINTHIANS 1:22

Being confident of this very thing, that He who has begun a good work in you will complete it until the day of Jesus Christ.

PHILIPPIANS 1:6

I am persuaded that neither death nor life, nor angels nor principalities nor powers, nor things present nor things to come, nor height nor depth, nor any other created thing, shall be able to separate us from the love of God which is in Christ Jesus our Lord.

ROMANS 8:38, 39

All that the Father gives Me will come to Me, and the one who comes to Me I will by no means cast out.

JOHN 6:37

Now to Him who is able to keep you from stumbling, and to present you faultless before the presence of His glory with exceeding joy, to God our Savior, who alone is wise, be glory and majesty, dominion and power, both now and forever. Amen.

JUDE 24, 25

Do not grieve the Holy Spirit of God, by whom you were sealed for the day of redemption.

EPHESIANS 4:30

Lift up your eyes on high,
And see who has created these things,
Who brings out their host by number;
He calls them all by name,
By the greatness of His might
And the strength of His power;
Not one is missing.

ISAIAH 40:26

Surely goodness and mercy shall follow me all the days of my life; and I will dwell in the house of the LORD forever.

PSALM 23:6

Do not labor for the food which perishes, but for the food which endures to everlasting life, which the Son of Man will give you, because God the Father has set His seal on Him.

JOHN 6:27

In Him you also trusted, after you heard the word of truth, the gospel of your salvation; in whom also, having believed, you were sealed with the Holy Spirit of promise.

EPHESIANS 1:13

JESUS IS YOUR SUFFICIENCY

God is able to make all grace abound toward you, that you, always having all sufficiency in all things, may have an abundance for every good work.

2 CORINTHIANS 9:8

My God shall supply all your need according to His riches in glory by Christ Jesus.

PHILIPPIANS 4:19

Therefore I say to you, whatever things you ask when you pray, believe that you receive them, and you will have them.

MARK 11:24

Not that we are sufficient of ourselves to think of anything as being from ourselves, but our sufficiency is from God.

2 CORINTHIANS 3:5

What is the exceeding greatness of His power toward us who believe, according to the working of His mighty power.

EPHESIANS 1:19

I can do all things through Christ who strengthens me.

PHILIPPIANS 4:13

He said to me, "My grace is sufficient for you, for My strength is made perfect in weakness." Therefore most gladly I will rather boast in my infirmities, that the power of Christ may rest upon me.

2 CORINTHIANS 12:9

Yet in all these things we are more than conquerors through Him who loved us.

ROMANS 8:37

Blessed be the God and Father of our Lord Jesus Christ, who has blessed us with every spiritual blessing in the heavenly places in Christ.

EPHESIANS 1:3

He who did not spare His own Son, but delivered Him up for us all, how shall He not with Him also freely give us all things?

ROMANS 8:32

Whatever you ask in My name, that I will do, that the Father may be glorified in the Son.

JOHN 14:13

In that day you will ask Me nothing. Most assuredly, I say to you, whatever you ask the Father in My name He will give you.

Until now you have asked nothing in My name. Ask, and you will receive, that your joy may be full.

JOHN 16:23, 24

His divine power has given to us all things that pertain to life and godliness, through the knowledge of Him who called us by glory and virtue, by which have been given to us exceedingly great and precious promises, that through these you may be partakers of the divine nature, having escaped the corruption that is in the world through lust.

2 PETER 1:3, 4

Bless the LORD, O my soul,
And forget not all His benefits:
Who forgives all your iniquities,
Who heals all your diseases,
Who redeems your life from destruction,
Who crowns you with lovingkindness and tender mercies.

PSALM 103:2–4

JESUS IS YOUR FULFILLMENT

Blessed are those who hunger and thirst for righteousness, for they shall be filled.

MATTHEW 5:6

Delight yourself also in the LORD, and He shall give you the desires of your heart.

PSALM 37:4

Who satisfies your mouth with good things, so that your youth is renewed like the eagle's.

PSALM 103:5

You shall eat in plenty and be satisfied,
And praise the name of the LORD your God,
Who has dealt wondrously with you;
And My people shall never be put to shame.

JOEL 2:26

My soul shall be satisfied as with marrow and fatness,
And my mouth shall praise You with joyful lips.
When I remember You on my bed,
I meditate on You in the night watches.

PSALM 63:5, 6

Jesus said to them, "I am the bread of life. He who comes to Me shall never hunger, and he who believes in Me shall never thirst."

JOHN 6:35

The poor shall eat and be satisfied;
Those who seek Him will praise the LORD.
Let your heart live forever!

PSALM 22:26

Jesus answered and said to her, "Whoever drinks of this water will thirst again, but whoever drinks of the water that I shall give him will never thirst. But the water that I shall give him will become in him a fountain of water springing up into everlasting life."

JOHN 4:13, 14

The LORD will answer and say to His people, "Behold, I will send you grain and new wine and oil, and you will be satisfied by them; I will no longer make you a reproach among the nations."

JOEL 2:19

"I will satiate the soul of the priests with abundance, and My people shall be satisfied with My goodness," says the LORD.

JEREMIAH 31:14

God's Promises

If you extend your soul to the hungry
And satisfy the afflicted soul,
Then your light shall dawn in the darkness,
And your darkness shall be as the noonday.
The LORD will guide you continually,
And satisfy your soul in drought,
And strengthen your bones;
You shall be like a watered garden,
And like a spring of water, whose waters do not fail.

ISAIAH 58:10, 11

The eyes of all look expectantly to You,
And You give them their food in due season.
You open Your hand
And satisfy the desire of every living thing.

PSALM 145:15, 16

Why do you spend money for what is not bread,
And your wages for what does not satisfy?
Listen carefully to Me, and eat what is good,
And let your soul delight itself in abundance.

ISAIAH 55:2

Jesus Is Your Everything

I can do all things through Christ who strengthens me.

PHILIPPIANS 4:13

My God shall supply all your need according to His riches in glory by Christ Jesus.

PHILIPPIANS 4:19

Yet in all these things we are more than conquerors through Him who loved us.

ROMANS 8:37

Therefore let no one boast in men. For all things are yours: whether Paul or Apollos or Cephas, or the world or life or death, or things present or things to come—all are yours.

And you are Christ's, and Christ is God's.

1 CORINTHIANS 3:21–23

Whatever we ask we receive from Him, because we keep His commandments and do those things that are pleasing in His sight.

1 JOHN 3:22

For to me, to live is Christ, and to die is gain.

PHILIPPIANS 1:21

Now to Him who is able to do exceedingly abundantly above all that we ask or think, according to the power that works in us, to Him be glory in the church by Christ Jesus to all generations, forever and ever. Amen.

EPHESIANS 3:20, 21

God is able to make all grace abound toward you, that you, always having all sufficiency in all things, may have an abundance for every good work.

2 CORINTHIANS 9:8

Blessed be the LORD,
Who daily loads us with benefits,
The God of our salvation!

PSALM 68:19

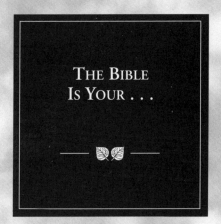

THE BIBLE
IS YOUR . . .

The Bible Is Your Infallible Authority

All Scripture is given by inspiration of God, and is profitable for doctrine, for reproof, for correction, for instruction in righteousness.

2 Timothy 3:16

Knowing this first, that no prophecy of Scripture is of any private interpretation, for prophecy never came by the will of man, but holy men of God spoke as they were moved by the Holy Spirit.

2 Peter 1:20, 21

For the word of God is living and powerful, and sharper than any two-edged sword, piercing even to the division of soul and spirit, and of joints and marrow, and is a discerner of the thoughts and intents of the heart.

Hebrews 4:12

By the word of the Lord the heavens were made, and all the host of them by the breath of His mouth.

Psalm 33:6

Forever, O LORD, your word is settled in heaven.

PSALM 119:89

For as the rain comes down, and the snow from heaven,
And do not return there,
But water the earth,
And make it bring forth and bud,
That it may give seed to the sower
And bread to the eater,
So shall My word be that goes forth from My mouth;
It shall not return to Me void,
But it shall accomplish what I please,
And it shall prosper in the thing for which I sent it.

ISAIAH 55:10, 11

You search the Scriptures, for in them you think you
have eternal life; and these are they which testify of
Me.

JOHN 5:39

Having been born again, not of corruptible seed but
incorruptible, through the word of God which lives
and abides forever.

1 PETER 1:23

By the word of the LORD the heavens were made, and all the host of them by the breath of His mouth.

PSALM 33:6

He spoke, and it was done; He commanded, and it stood fast.

PSALM 33:9

Where is the wise? Where is the scribe? Where is the disputer of this age? Has not God made foolish the wisdom of this world?

1 CORINTHIANS 1:20

"All flesh is as grass,
  And all the glory of man as the flower of the grass.
  The grass withers,
  And its flower falls away,
  But the word of the LORD endures forever."
  Now this is the word which by the gospel was preached
    to you.

1 PETER 1:24, 25

Heaven and earth will pass away, but My words will by no means pass away.

MARK 13:31

THE BIBLE IS YOUR DEED
OF INHERITANCE

So now, brethren, I commend you to God and to the word of His grace, which is able to build you up and give you an inheritance among all those who are sanctified.

ACTS 20:32

To open their eyes, in order to turn them from darkness to light, and from the power of Satan to God, that they may receive forgiveness of sins and an inheritance among those who are sanctified by faith in Me.

ACTS 26:18

The Spirit Himself bears witness with our spirit that we are children of God, and if children, then heirs—heirs of God and joint heirs with Christ, if indeed we suffer with Him, that we may also be glorified together.

ROMANS 8:16, 17

If you are Christ's, then you are Abraham's seed, and heirs according to the promise.

GALATIANS 3:29

That the Gentiles should be fellow heirs, of the same body, and partakers of His promise in Christ through the gospel.

EPHESIANS 3:6

In My Father's house are many mansions; if it were not so, I would have told you. I go to prepare a place for you.

And if I go and prepare a place for you, I will come again and receive you to Myself; that where I am, there you may be also.

JOHN 14:2, 3

Then the King will say to those on His right hand, "Come, you blessed of My Father, inherit the kingdom prepared for you from the foundation of the world."

MATTHEW 25:34

For all the promises of God in Him are Yes, and in Him Amen, to the glory of God through us.

2 CORINTHIANS 1:20

But as it is written:
"Eye has not seen, nor ear heard,
  Nor have entered into the heart of man
  The things which God has prepared for those who
    love Him."

1 Corinthians 2:9

Whatever you do, do it heartily, as to the Lord and
not to men, knowing that from the Lord you will
receive the reward of the inheritance; for you serve
the Lord Christ.

Colossians 3:23, 24

Wait on the Lord,
And keep His way,
And He shall exalt you to inherit the land;
When the wicked are cut off, you shall see it.

Psalm 37:34

THE BIBLE IS YOUR
GUIDE FOR LIFE

Your word is a lamp to my feet and a light to my path.

PSALM 119:105

When you roam, they will lead you;
When you sleep, they will keep you;
And when you awake, they will speak with you.
For the commandment is a lamp,
And the law a light;
Reproofs of instruction are the way of life.

PROVERBS 6:22, 23

Your word I have hidden in my heart, that I might not sin against You.

PSALM 119:11

Moreover by them Your servant is warned, and in keeping them there is great reward.

PSALM 19:11

How can a young man cleanse his way? By taking heed according to Your word.

PSALM 119:9

Your testimonies also are my delight and my counselors.

PSALM 119:24

By which have been given to us exceedingly great and precious promises, that through these you may be partakers of the divine nature, having escaped the corruption that is in the world through lust.

2 PETER 1:4

The steps of a good man are ordered by the LORD, and He delights in his way.

PSALM 37:23

I will instruct you and teach you in the way you should go; I will guide you with My eye.

PSALM 32:8

He restores my soul; He leads me in the paths of righteousness for His name's sake.

PSALM 23:3

Your ears shall hear a word behind you, saying,
"This is the way, walk in it,"
  Whenever you turn to the right hand
  Or whenever you turn to the left.

ISAIAH 30:21

As He spoke by the mouth of His holy prophets, who
have been since the world began, . . . to give light to
those who sit in darkness and the shadow of death, to
guide our feet into the way of peace.

LUKE 1:70, 79

This Book of the Law shall not depart from your
mouth, but you shall meditate in it day and night,
that you may observe to do according to all that is
written in it. For then you will make your way prosperous, and then you will have good success.

JOSHUA 1:8

THE BIBLE IS YOUR STABILITY

That He would grant you, according to the riches of His glory, to be strengthened with might through His Spirit in the inner man.

EPHESIANS 3:16

Forever, O LORD, Your word is settled in heaven.

PSALM 119:89

The grass withers, the flower fades, but the word of our God stands forever.

ISAIAH 40:8

For assuredly, I say to you, till heaven and earth pass away, one jot or one tittle will by no means pass from the law till all is fulfilled.

MATTHEW 5:18

He also brought me up out of a horrible pit,
Out of the miry clay,
And set my feet upon a rock,
And established my steps.

PSALM 40:2

God's Promises

My son, give attention to my words;
Incline your ear to my sayings.
Do not let them depart from your eyes;
Keep them in the midst of your heart;
For they are life to those who find them,
And health to all their flesh.

PROVERBS 4:20–22

Blessed be the LORD, who has given rest to His people Israel, according to all that He promised. There has not failed one word of all His good promise, which He promised through His servant Moses.

1 KINGS 8:56

"I am the LORD. I speak, and the word which I speak will come to pass; it will no more be postponed; for in your days, O rebellious house, I will say the word and perform it," says the Lord GOD.

EZEKIEL 12:25

What then shall we say to these things? If God is for us, who can be against us?

ROMANS 8:31

And he said, "O man greatly beloved, fear not! Peace be to you; be strong, yes, be strong!" So when he spoke to me I was strengthened, and said, "Let my lord speak, for you have strengthened me."

DANIEL 10:19

My soul melts from heaviness; strengthen me according to Your word.

PSALM 119:28

For thus says the Lord GOD, the Holy One of Israel: "In returning and rest you shall be saved; in quietness and confidence shall be your strength."

ISAIAH 30:15

God is our refuge and strength, a very present help in trouble.

PSALM 46:1

The name of the LORD is a strong tower; the righteous run to it and are safe.

PROVERBS 18:10

But those who wait on the LORD
Shall renew their strength;
They shall mount up with wings like eagles,
They shall run and not be weary,
They shall walk and not faint.

ISAIAH 40:31

That you may walk worthy of the Lord, fully pleasing Him, being fruitful in every good work and increasing in the knowledge of God; strengthened with all might, according to His glorious power, for all patience and longsuffering with joy; giving thanks to the Father who has qualified us to be partakers of the inheritance of the saints in the light.

COLOSSIANS 1:10–12

Then he said to them, "Go your way, eat the fat, drink the sweet, and send portions to those for whom nothing is prepared; for this day is holy to our LORD. Do not sorrow, for the joy of the LORD is your strength."

NEHEMIAH 8:10

Fear not, for I am with you;
Be not dismayed, for I am your God.
I will strengthen you,
Yes, I will help you,
I will uphold you with My righteous right hand.

ISAIAH 41:10

Counsel is mine, and sound wisdom; I am understanding, I have strength.

PROVERBS 8:14

He gives power to the weak, and to those who have no might He increases strength.

ISAIAH 40:29

The LORD is my rock and my fortress and my deliverer;
My God, my strength, in whom I will trust;
My shield and the horn of my salvation, my stronghold.

PSALM 18:2

Therefore take up the whole armor of God, that you may be able to withstand in the evil day, and having done all, to stand.

EPHESIANS 6:13

WHAT TO DO WHEN
YOU FEEL . . .

WHAT TO DO WHEN YOU
FEEL DISCOURAGED

So the ransomed of the LORD shall return,
And come to Zion with singing,
With everlasting joy on their heads.
They shall obtain joy and gladness;
Sorrow and sighing shall flee away.

ISAIAH 51:11

In this you greatly rejoice, though now for a little while, if need be, you have been grieved by various trials, that the genuineness of your faith, being much more precious than gold that perishes, though it is tested by fire, may be found to praise, honor, and glory at the revelation of Jesus Christ, whom having not seen you love.

Though now you do not see Him, yet believing, you rejoice with joy inexpressible and full of glory, receiving the end of your faith—the salvation of your souls.

1 PETER 1:6–9

Let not your heart be troubled; you believe in God, believe also in Me.

JOHN 14:1

Though I walk in the midst of trouble, You will revive
   me;
You will stretch out Your hand
Against the wrath of my enemies,
And Your right hand will save me.

PSALM 138:7

The LORD is my light and my salvation;
Whom shall I fear?
The LORD is the strength of my life;
Of whom shall I be afraid?
When the wicked came against me
To eat up my flesh,
My enemies and foes,
They stumbled and fell.
Though an army may encamp against me,
My heart shall not fear;
Though war may rise against me,
In this I will be confident.

PSALM 27:1–3

WHAT TO DO WHEN YOU FEEL WORRIED

Casting all your care upon Him, for He cares for you.

1 PETER 5:7

Be anxious for nothing, but in everything by prayer and supplication, with thanksgiving, let your requests be made known to God; and the peace of God, which surpasses all understanding, will guard your hearts and minds through Christ Jesus.

PHILIPPIANS 4:6, 7

Let the peace of God rule in your hearts, to which also you were called in one body; and be thankful.

COLOSSIANS 3:15

You will keep him in perfect peace, whose mind is stayed on You, because he trusts in You.

ISAIAH 26:3

To be carnally minded is death, but to be spiritually minded is life and peace.

ROMANS 8:6

Therefore I say to you, do not worry about your life, what you will eat or what you will drink; nor about your body, what you will put on. Is not life more than food and the body more than clothing?

Look at the birds of the air, for they neither sow nor reap nor gather into barns; yet your heavenly Father feeds them. Are you not of more value than they?

Which of you by worrying can add one cubit to his stature?

So why do you worry about clothing? Consider the lilies of the field, how they grow: they neither toil nor spin; and yet I say to you that even Solomon in all his glory was not arrayed like one of these.

Now if God so clothes the grass of the field, which today is, and tomorrow is thrown into the oven, will He not much more clothe you, O you of little faith?

Therefore do not worry, saying, "What shall we eat?" or "What shall we drink?" or "What shall we wear?"

For after all these things the Gentiles seek. For your heavenly Father knows that you need all these things.

MATTHEW 6:25–32

I will both lie down in peace, and sleep; for You alone, O LORD, make me dwell in safety.

PSALM 4:8

My God shall supply all your need according to His riches in glory by Christ Jesus.

PHILIPPIANS 4:19

When you lie down, you will not be afraid; Yes, you will lie down and your sleep will be sweet.

PROVERBS 3:24

For we who have believed do enter that rest, as He has said: "So I swore in My wrath, 'They shall not enter My rest,'" although the works were finished from the foundation of the world.

There remains therefore a rest for the people of God.

HEBREWS 4:3, 9

What to Do When You Feel Lonely

Let your conduct be without covetousness; be content with such things as you have. For He Himself has said, "I will never leave you nor forsake you."

HEBREWS 13:5

Teaching them to observe all things that I have commanded you; and lo, I am with you always, even to the end of the age. Amen.

MATTHEW 28:20

The eternal God is your refuge,
And underneath are the everlasting arms;
He will thrust out the enemy from before you,
And will say, "Destroy!"

DEUTERONOMY 33:27

Fear not, for I am with you;
Be not dismayed, for I am your God.
I will strengthen you,
Yes, I will help you,
I will uphold you with My righteous right hand.

ISAIAH 41:10

Be strong and of good courage, do not fear nor be afraid of them; for the LORD your God, He is the One who goes with you. He will not leave you nor forsake you.

DEUTERONOMY 31:6

The LORD will not forsake His people, for His great name's sake, because it has pleased the LORD to make you His people.

1 SAMUEL 12:22

I will not leave you orphans; I will come to you.

JOHN 14:18

Let not your heart be troubled; you believe in God, believe also in Me.

JOHN 14:1

He heals the brokenhearted and binds up their wounds.

PSALM 147:3

(For the LORD your God is a merciful God), He will not forsake you nor destroy you, nor forget the covenant of your fathers which He swore to them.

DEUTERONOMY 4:31

When my father and my mother forsake me,
Then the LORD will take care of me.

PSALM 27:10

"For the mountains shall depart
And the hills be removed,
But My kindness shall not depart from you,
Nor shall My covenant of peace be removed,"
Says the LORD, who has mercy on you.

ISAIAH 54:10

Casting all your care upon Him, for He cares for you.

1 PETER 5:7

God is our refuge and strength,
A very present help in trouble.

PSALM 46:1

What to Do When You Feel Depressed

Finally, brethren, whatever things are true, whatever things are noble, whatever things are just, whatever things are pure, whatever things are lovely, whatever things are of good report, if there is any virtue and if there is anything praiseworthy—meditate on these things.

PHILIPPIANS 4:8

Beloved, do not think it strange concerning the fiery trial which is to try you, as though some strange thing happened to you; but rejoice to the extent that you partake of Christ's sufferings, that when His glory is revealed, you may also be glad with exceeding joy.

1 PETER 4:12, 13

To console those who mourn in Zion,
To give them beauty for ashes,
The oil of joy for mourning,
The garment of praise for the spirit of heaviness;
That they may be called trees of righteousness,
The planting of the LORD, that He may be glorified.

ISAIAH 61:3

The righteous cry out, and the LORD hears, and delivers them out of all their troubles.

PSALM 34:17

Fear not, for I am with you;
Be not dismayed, for I am your God.
I will strengthen you,
Yes, I will help you,
I will uphold you with My righteous right hand.

ISAIAH 41:10

Blessed be the God and Father of our Lord Jesus Christ, the Father of mercies and God of all comfort, who comforts us in all our tribulation, that we may be able to comfort those who are in any trouble, with the comfort with which we ourselves are comforted by God.

2 CORINTHIANS 1:3, 4

For His anger is but for a moment,
His favor is for life;
Weeping may endure for a night,
But joy comes in the morning.

PSALM 30:5

WHAT TO DO WHEN YOU FEEL DISSATISFIED

The young lions lack and suffer hunger; but those who seek the LORD shall not lack any good thing.

PSALM 34:10

I will pour water on him who is thirsty,
And floods on the dry ground;
I will pour My Spirit on your descendants,
And My blessing on your offspring.

ISAIAH 44:3

A man will be satisfed with good by the fruit of his mouth, and the recompense of a man's hands will be rendered to him.

PROVERBS 12:14

I know how to be abased, and I know how to abound. Everywhere and in all things I have learned both to be full and to be hungry, both to abound and to suffer need.

I can do all things through Christ who strengthens me.

PHILIPPIANS 4:12, 13

O God, You are my God;
Early will I seek You;
My soul thirsts for You;
My flesh longs for You . . . .
So I have looked for You in the sanctuary,
To see Your power and Your glory.
Because Your lovingkindness is better than life,
My lips shall praise You.
Thus I will bless You while I live;
I will lift up my hands in Your name.
My soul shall be satisfied as with marrow and fatness,
And my mouth shall praise You with joyful lips.

PSALM 63:1–5

Blessed are those who hunger and thirst for righteousness, for they shall be filled.

MATTHEW 5:6

Trust in the LORD, and do good; dwell in the land,
and feed on His faithfulness.

PSALM 37:3

He satisfies the longing soul, and fills the hungry soul
with goodness.

PSALM 107:9

What to Do When You Feel Dissatisfied

Ho! Everyone who thirsts,
Come to the waters;
And you who have no money,
Come, buy and eat.
Yes, come, buy wine and milk
Without money and without price.

ISAIAH 55:1

God is able to make all grace abound toward you,
that you, always having all sufficiency in all things,
may have an abundance for every good work.

2 CORINTHIANS 9:8

Bless the LORD, O my soul,
And forget not all His benefits:
Who forgives all your iniquities,
Who heals all your diseases,
Who redeems your life from destruction,
Who crowns you with lovingkindness and tender
   mercies,
Who satisfies your mouth with good things,
So that your youth is renewed like the eagle's.

PSALM 103:2–5

What to Do When You Feel Condemned

There is therefore now no condemnation to those who are in Christ Jesus, who do not walk according to the flesh, but according to the Spirit.

ROMANS 8:1

He has not dealt with us according to our sins,
Nor punished us according to our iniquities.
As far as the east is from the west,
So far has He removed our transgressions from us.

PSALM 103:10, 12

Therefore, if anyone is in Christ, he is a new creation; old things have passed away; behold, all things have become new.

2 CORINTHIANS 5:17

God did not send His Son into the world to condemn the world, but that the world through Him might be saved.

He who believes in Him is not condemned; but he who does not believe is condemned already, because he has not believed in the name of the only begotten Son of God.

JOHN 3:17, 18

Most assuredly, I say to you, he who hears My word and believes in Him who sent Me has everlasting life, and shall not come into judgment, but has passed from death into life.

JOHN 5:24

I will be merciful to their unrighteousness, and their sins and their lawless deeds I will remember no more.

HEBREWS 8:12

I, even I, am He who blots out your transgressions for My own sake; and I will not remember your sins.

ISAIAH 43:25

God's Promises

Let the wicked forsake his way,
And the unrighteous man his thoughts;
Let him return to the LORD,
And He will have mercy on him;
And to our God,
For He will abundantly pardon.

ISAIAH 55:7

I acknowledged my sin to You,
And my iniquity I have not hidden.
I said, "I will confess my transgressions to the LORD,"
And You forgave the iniquity of my sin.

PSALM 32:5

If we confess our sins, He is faithful and just to forgive
us our sins and to cleanse us from all unrighteousness.

1 JOHN 1:9

Blessed is he whose transgression is forgiven, whose
sin is covered.

PSALM 32:1

Let us draw near with a true heart in full assurance of
faith, having our hearts sprinkled from an evil conscience and our bodies washed with pure water.

HEBREWS 10:22

WHAT TO DO WHEN YOU FEEL CONFUSED

God is not the author of confusion but of peace, as in all the churches of the saints.

1 CORINTHIANS 14:33

For God has not given us a spirit of fear, but of power and of love and of a sound mind.

2 TIMOTHY 1:7

For where envy and self-seeking exist, confusion and every evil thing are there.

But the wisdom that is from above is first pure, then peaceable, gentle, willing to yield, full of mercy and good fruits, without partiality and without hypocrisy.

Now the fruit of righteousness is sown in peace by those who make peace.

JAMES 3:16–18

The Lord GOD will help Me; therefore I will not be disgraced; therefore I have set My face like a flint, and I know that I will not be ashamed.

ISAIAH 50:7

If any of you lacks wisdom, let him ask of God, who gives to all liberally and without reproach, and it will be given to him.

JAMES 1:5

Trust in the LORD with all your heart,
And lean not on your own understanding;
In all your ways acknowledge Him,
And He shall direct your paths.

PROVERBS 3:5, 6

I will instruct you and teach you in the way you should go; I will guide you with My eye.

PSALM 32:8

Great peace have those who love Your law, and nothing causes them to stumble.

PSALM 119:165

Cast your burden on the LORD, and He shall sustain you; He shall never permit the righteous to be moved.

PSALM 55:22

WHAT TO DO WHEN YOU FEEL TEMPTED

Let him who thinks he stands take heed lest he fall.

No temptation has overtaken you except such as is common to man; but God is faithful, who will not allow you to be tempted beyond what you are able, but with the temptation will also make the way of escape, that you may be able to bear it.

1 CORINTHIANS 10:12, 13

Seeing then that we have a great High Priest who has passed through the heavens, Jesus the Son of God, let us hold fast our confession.

For we do not have a High Priest who cannot sympathize with our weaknesses, but was in all points tempted as we are, yet without sin.

Let us therefore come boldly to the throne of grace, that we may obtain mercy and find grace to help in time of need.

HEBREWS 4:14–16

Submit to God. Resist the devil and he will flee from you.

JAMES 4:7

In that He Himself has suffered, being tempted, He is able to aid those who are tempted.

HEBREWS 2:18

Sin shall not have dominion over you, for you are not under law but under grace.

ROMANS 6:14

Your word I have hidden in my heart, that I might not sin against You.

PSALM 119:11

Let no one say when he is tempted, "I am tempted by God"; for God cannot be tempted by evil, nor does He Himself tempt anyone.

But each one is tempted when he is drawn away by his own desires and enticed.

JAMES 1:13, 14

Be sober, be vigilant; because your adversary the devil walks about like a roaring lion, seeking whom he may devour.

Resist him, steadfast in the faith, knowing that the same sufferings are experienced by your brotherhood in the world.

1 PETER 5:8, 9

Finally, my brethren, be strong in the Lord and in the power of His might.

Put on the whole armor of God, that you may be able to stand against the wiles of the devil.

Above all, [take] the shield of faith with which you will be able to quench all the fiery darts of the wicked one.

EPHESIANS 6:10, 11, 16

You are of God, little children, and have overcome them, because He who is in you is greater than he who is in the world.

1 JOHN 4:4

Blessed is the man who endures temptation; for when he has been approved, he will receive the crown of life which the Lord has promised to those who love Him.

JAMES 1:12

The Lord knows how to deliver the godly out of temptations and to reserve the unjust under punishment for the day of judgment.

2 PETER 2:9

What to Do When You Feel Angry

So then, my beloved brethren, let every man be swift to hear, slow to speak, slow to wrath; for the wrath of man does not produce the righteousness of God.

JAMES 1:19, 20

"Be angry, and do not sin": do not let the sun go down on your wrath.

EPHESIANS 4:26

A soft answer turns away wrath, but a harsh word stirs up anger.

PROVERBS 15:1

If you forgive men their trespasses, your heavenly Father will also forgive you.

MATTHEW 6:14

If your enemy is hungry, give him bread to eat;
And if he is thirsty, give him water to drink;
For so you will heap coals of fire on his head,
And the LORD will reward you.

PROVERBS 25:21, 22

Beloved, do not avenge yourselves, but rather give place to wrath; for it is written, "Vengeance is Mine, I will repay," says the Lord.

ROMANS 12:19

He who is slow to wrath has great understanding,
But he who is impulsive exalts folly.

PROVERBS 14:29

He who is slow to anger is better than the mighty,
And he who rules his spirit than he who takes a
  city.

PROVERBS 16:32

Do not hasten in your spirit to be angry,
For anger rests in the bosom of fools.

ECCLESIASTES 7:9

Cease from anger, and forsake wrath;
Do not fret—it only causes harm.

PSALM 37:8

Let all bitterness, wrath, anger, clamor, and evil speaking be put away from you, with all malice.

And be kind to one another, tenderhearted, forgiving one another, even as God in Christ forgave you.

EPHESIANS 4:31, 32

But I say to you that whoever is angry with his brother without a cause shall be in danger of the judgment. And whoever says to his brother, "Raca!" shall be in danger of the council. But whoever says, "You fool!" shall be in danger of hell fire.

Therefore if you bring your gift to the altar, and there remember that your brother has something against you, leave your gift there before the altar, and go your way. First be reconciled to your brother, and then come and offer your gift.

MATTHEW 5:22–24

A wise man fears and departs from evil,
But a fool rages and is self-confident.
A quick-tempered man acts foolishly,
And a man of wicked intentions is hated.

PROVERBS 14:16, 17

What to Do When You Feel Rebellious

Therefore gird up the loins of your mind, be sober, and rest your hope fully upon the grace that is to be brought to you at the revelation of Jesus Christ; as obedient children, not conforming yourselves to the former lusts, as in your ignorance.

1 PETER 1:13, 14

You younger people, submit yourselves to your elders. Yes, all of you be submissive to one another, and be clothed with humility, for "God resists the proud, but gives grace to the humble."

Therefore humble yourselves under the mighty hand of God, that He may exalt you in due time.

1 PETER 5:5, 6

Though He was a Son, yet He learned obedience by the things which He suffered.

HEBREWS 5:8

Submit to God. Resist the devil and he will flee from you.

JAMES 4:7

Submitting to one another in the fear of God.

EPHESIANS 5:21

No grave trouble will overtake the righteous, but the wicked shall be filled with evil.

PROVERBS 12:21

For rebellion is as the sin of witchcraft, and stubbornness is as iniquity and idolatry.

1 SAMUEL 15:23

Submit yourselves to every ordinance of man for the Lord's sake, whether to the king as supreme, or to governors, as to those who are sent by him for the punishment of evildoers and for the praise of those who do good.

For this is the will of God, that by doing good you may put to silence the ignorance of foolish men.

1 PETER 2:13–15

Obey those who rule over you, and be submissive, for they watch out for your souls, as those who must give account. Let them do so with joy and not with grief, for that would be unprofitable for you.

HEBREWS 13:17

WHAT TO DO WHEN YOUR ARE . . .

WHAT TO DO WHEN YOU ARE
EXPERIENCING FEAR

He shall cover you with His feathers,
And under His wings you shall take refuge;
His truth shall be your shield and buckler.
You shall not be afraid of the terror by night,
Nor of the arrow that flies by day,
Nor of the pestilence that walks in darkness,
Nor of the destruction that lays waste at noonday.
A thousand may fall at your side,
And ten thousand at your right hand;
But it shall not come near you.

PSALM 91:4–7

Do not be afraid of sudden terror,
Nor of trouble from the wicked when it comes;
For the LORD will be your confidence,
And will keep your foot from being caught.

PROVERBS 3:25, 26

You did not receive the spirit of bondage again to fear,
but you received the Spirit of adoption by whom we
cry out, "Abba, Father."

ROMANS 8:15

What to Do When You Are Experiencing Fear

The LORD is my light and my salvation;
Whom shall I fear?
The LORD is the strength of my life;
Of whom shall I be afraid? . . .
Though an army may encamp against me,
My heart shall not fear;
Though war should rise against me,
In this I will be confident.

PSALM 27:1, 3

Yea, though I walk through the valley of the shadow
    of death,
I will fear no evil;
For You are with me;
Your rod and Your staff, they comfort me.
You prepare a table before me in the presence of my
    enemies;
You anoint my head with oil;
My cup runs over.

PSALM 23:4, 5

No evil shall befall you,
Nor shall any plague come near your dwelling;
For He shall give His angels charge over you,
To keep you in all your ways.

PSALM 91:10, 11

There is no fear in love; but perfect love casts out fear, because fear involves torment. But he who fears has not been made perfect in love.

1 JOHN 4:18

In righteousness you shall be established; you shall be far from oppression, for you shall not fear; and from terror, for it shall not come near you.

ISAIAH 54:14

He who dwells in the secret place of the Most High Shall abide under the shadow of the Almighty.

PSALM 91:1

In God I have put my trust; I will not be afraid. What can man do to me?

PSALM 56:11

Be of good courage,
And He shall strengthen your heart,
All you who hope in the LORD.

PSALM 31:24

WHAT TO DO WHEN YOU ARE EMOTIONALLY DISTRAUGHT

God has not given us a spirit of fear, but of power and of love and of a sound mind.

2 TIMOTHY 1:7

Fear not, for I am with you;
Be not dismayed, for I am your God.
I will strengthen you,
Yes, I will help you,
I will uphold you with My righteous right hand.

ISAIAH 41:10

God is not the author of confusion but of peace, as in all the churches of the saints.

1 CORINTHIANS 14:33

Blessed be the God and Father of our Lord Jesus Christ, the Father of mercies and God of all comfort, who comforts us in all our tribulation, that we may be able to comfort those who are in any trouble, with the comfort with which we ourselves are comforted by God.

2 CORINTHIANS 1:3, 4

Where envy and self-seeking exist, confusion and every evil thing are there.

But the wisdom that is from above is first pure, then peaceable, gentle, willing to yield, full of mercy and good fruits, without partiality and without hypocrisy.

Now the fruit of righteousness is sown in peace by those who make peace.

JAMES 3:16–18

Cast your burden on the LORD, and He shall sustain you; He shall never permit the righteous to be moved.

PSALM 55:22

Great peace have those who love Your law, and nothing causes them to stumble.

PSALM 119:165

When you pass through the waters, I will be with you;
And through the rivers, they shall not overflow you.
When you walk through the fire, you shall not be burned,
Nor shall the flame scorch you.

ISAIAH 43:2

What to Do When You Are in Need of Courage

Wait on the LORD;
Be of good courage,
And He shall strengthen your heart;
Wait, I say, on the LORD!

PSALM 27:14

Beloved, do not think it strange concerning the fiery trial which is to try you, as though some strange thing happened to you; but rejoice to the extent that you partake of Christ's sufferings, that when His glory is revealed, you may also be glad with exceeding joy.

1 PETER 4:12, 13

I am persuaded that neither death nor life, nor angels nor principalities nor powers, nor things present nor things to come, nor height nor depth, nor any other created thing, shall be able to separate us from the love of God which is in Christ Jesus our Lord.

ROMANS 8:38, 39

Fear not, for I am with you;
Be not dismayed, for I am your God.
I will strengthen you,
Yes, I will help you,
I will uphold you with My righteous right hand.

ISAIAH 41:10

The eternal God is your refuge, and underneath are the everlasting arms; He will thrust out the enemy from before you, and will say, "Destroy!"

DEUTERONOMY 33:27

I shall not die, but live, and declare the works of the LORD.

PSALM 118:17

I can do all things through Christ who strengthens me.

PHILIPPIANS 4:13

Be of good courage, and He shall strengthen your heart, all you who hope in the LORD.

PSALM 31:24

What to Do When You Are in Need of Courage

Those who wait on the LORD
Shall renew their strength;
They shall mount up with wings like eagles,
They shall run and not be weary,
They shall walk and not faint.

ISAIAH 40:31

So the ransomed of the LORD shall return,
And come to Zion with singing,
With everlasting joy on their heads.
They shall obtain joy and gladness;
Sorrow and sighing shall flee away.

ISAIAH 51:11

What to Do When You Are in Need of Patience

But the fruit of the Spirit is love, joy, peace, long-suffering, kindness, goodness, faithfulness.

GALATIANS 5:22

Knowing that the testing of your faith produces patience.
But let patience have its perfect work, that you may be perfect and complete, lacking nothing.

JAMES 1:3, 4

Do not become sluggish, but imitate those who through faith and patience inherit the promises.

HEBREWS 6:12

It is good that one should hope and wait quietly for the salvation of the LORD.

LAMENTATIONS 3:26

If we hope for what we do not see, we eagerly wait for it with perseverance.

ROMANS 8:25

What to Do When You Are in Need of Patience

The end of a thing is better than its beginning;
The patient in spirit is better than the proud in spirit.
Do not hasten in your spirit to be angry,
For anger rests in the bosom of fools.

ECCLESIASTES 7:8, 9

Whatever things were written before were written for our learning, that we through the patience and comfort of the Scriptures might have hope.

Now may the God of patience and comfort grant you to be like-minded toward one another, according to Christ Jesus.

ROMANS 15:4, 5

Rest in the LORD, and wait patiently for Him;
Do not fret because of him who prospers in his way,
Because of the man who brings wicked schemes to
    pass.

PSALM 37:7

I waited patiently for the LORD; and He inclined to me, and heard my cry.

PSALM 40:1

Do not cast away your confidence, which has great reward.

For you have need of endurance, so that after you have done the will of God, you may receive the promise: "For yet a little while, and He who is coming will come and will not tarry."

HEBREWS 10:35–37

Since we are surrounded by so great a cloud of witnesses, let us lay aside every weight, and the sin which so easily ensnares us, and let us run with endurance the race that is set before us.

HEBREWS 12:1

We also glory in tribulations, knowing that tribulation produces perseverance; and perseverance, character; and character, hope.

Now hope does not disappoint, because the love of God has been poured out in our hearts by the Holy Spirit who was given to us.

ROMANS 5:3–5

What to Do When You Are in Need of Peace

You will keep him in perfect peace, whose mind is stayed on You, because he trusts in You.

ISAIAH 26:3

Be anxious for nothing, but in everything by prayer and supplication, with thanksgiving, let your requests be made known to God; and the peace of God, which surpasses all understanding, will guard your hearts and minds through Christ Jesus.

PHILIPPIANS 4:6, 7

LORD, You will establish peace for us, for You have also done all our works in us.

ISAIAH 26:12

He shall enter into peace; they shall rest in their beds, each one walking in his uprightness.

ISAIAH 57:2

You shall go out with joy,
And be led out with peace;
The mountains and the hills
Shall break forth into singing before you,
And all the trees of the field shall clap their hands.

ISAIAH 55:12

Mark the blameless man, and observe the upright;
For the future of that man is peace.

PSALM 37:37

To be carnally minded is death, but to be spiritually minded is life and peace.

ROMANS 8:6

The kingdom of God is not eating and drinking, but righteousness and peace and joy in the Holy Spirit.

For he who serves Christ in these things is acceptable to God and approved by men.

Therefore let us pursue the things which make for peace and the things by which one may edify another.

ROMANS 14:17–19

Great peace have those who love Your law,
And nothing causes them to stumble.

PSALM 119:165

The meek shall inherit the earth,
And shall delight themselves in the abundance of
  peace.

PSALM 37:11

Finally, brethren, farewell. Become complete. Be of
good comfort, be of one mind, live in peace; and the
God of love and peace will be with you.

2 CORINTHIANS 13:11

May the God of hope fill you with all joy and peace
in believing, that you may abound in hope by the
power of the Holy Spirit.

ROMANS 15:13

What to Do When You Are Lukewarm Spiritually

Be watchful, and strengthen the things which remain, that are ready to die, for I have not found your works perfect before God.

I know your works, that you are neither cold nor hot. I could wish you were cold or hot.

So then, because you are lukewarm, and neither cold nor hot, I will vomit you out of My mouth.

REVELATION 3:2, 15, 16

I have this against you, that you have left your first love.

REVELATION 2:4

If we confess our sins, He is faithful and just to forgive us our sins and to cleanse us from all unrighteousness.

1 JOHN 1:9

Take heed to yourself, and diligently keep yourself, lest you forget the things your eyes have seen, and lest they depart from your heart all the days of your life. And teach them to your children and your grandchildren.

DEUTERONOMY 4:9

Beware that you do not forget the LORD your God by not keeping His commandments, His judgments, and His statutes which I command you today, lest—when you have eaten and are full, and have built beautiful houses and dwell in them; and when your herds and your flocks multiply, and your silver and your gold are multiplied, and all that you have is multiplied; when your heart is lifted up, and you forget the LORD your God who brought you out of the land of Egypt, from the house of bondage.

DEUTERONOMY 8:11–14

If we had forgotten the name of our God,
Or stretched out our hands to a foreign god,
Would not God search this out?
For He knows the secrets of the heart.

PSALM 44:20, 21

Beware, brethren, lest there be in any of you an evil heart of unbelief in departing from the living God; but exhort one another daily, while it is called "Today," lest any of you be hardened through the deceitfulness of sin.

HEBREWS 3:12, 13

Of whom we have much to say, and hard to explain, since you have become dull of hearing.

For though by this time you ought to be teachers, you need someone to teach you again the first principles of the oracles of God; and you have come to need milk and not solid food.

HEBREWS 5:11, 12

"Yet from the days of your fathers you have gone away from My ordinances and have not kept them. Return to Me, and I will return to you," says the LORD of hosts.

MALACHI 3:7

If, after they have escaped the pollutions of the world through the knowledge of the Lord and Savior Jesus Christ, they are again entangled in them and overcome, the latter end is worse for them than the beginning.

For it would have been better for them not to have known the way of righteousness, than having known it, to turn from the holy commandment delivered to them.

2 PETER 2:20, 21

WHAT TO DO WHEN YOU ARE GRIEVING

I do not want you to be ignorant, brethren, concerning those who have fallen asleep, lest you sorrow as others who have no hope.

For if we believe that Jesus died and rose again, even so God will bring with Him those who sleep in Jesus.

1 THESSALONIANS 4:13, 14

The LORD has comforted His people,
And will have mercy on His afflicted.

ISAIAH 49:13b

Blessed are those who mourn, for they shall be comforted.

MATTHEW 5:4

Blessed be the God and Father of our Lord Jesus Christ, the Father of mercies and God of all comfort, who comforts us in all our tribulation, that we may be able to comfort those who are in any trouble, with the comfort with which we ourselves are comforted by God.

2 CORINTHIANS 1:3, 4

This is my comfort in my affliction,
For Your word has given me life.

PSALM 119:50

O Death, where is your sting? O Hades, where is your
victory?
The sting of death is sin, and the strength of sin is the
law.
But thanks be to God, who gives us the victory
through our Lord Jesus Christ.

1 CORINTHIANS 15:55–57

Yea, though I walk through the valley of the shadow
of death,
I will fear no evil;
For You are with me;
Your rod and Your staff, they comfort me.

PSALM 23:4

God will wipe away every tear from their eyes; there
shall be no more death, nor sorrow, nor crying. There
shall be no more pain, for the former things have
passed away.

REVELATION 21:4

What to Do When You Are Grieving

Casting all your care upon Him, for He cares for you.

1 PETER 5:7

Fear not, for I am with you;
Be not dismayed, for I am your God.
I will strengthen you,
Yes, I will help you,
I will uphold you with My righteous right hand.

ISAIAH 41:10

WHAT TO DO WHEN YOU ARE DOUBTING GOD

Jesus answered and said to them, "Have faith in God.

"For assuredly, I say to you, whoever says to this mountain, 'Be removed and be cast into the sea,' and does not doubt in his heart, but believes that those things he says will be done, he will have whatever he says.

"Therefore I say to you, whatever things you ask when you pray, believe that you receive them, and you will have them."

MARK 11:22–24

Do not seek what you should eat or what you should drink, nor have an anxious mind.

For all these things the nations of the world seek after, and your Father knows that you need these things.

But seek the kingdom of God, and all these things shall be added to you.

LUKE 12:29–31

He who calls you is faithful, who also will do it.

1 THESSALONIANS 5:24

He did not waver at the promise of God through unbelief, but was strengthened in faith, giving glory to God, and being fully convinced that what He had promised He was also able to perform.

ROMANS 4:20, 21

> My counsel shall stand,
> And I will do all My pleasure . . .
> Indeed I have spoken it;
> I will also bring it to pass.
> I have purposed it;
> I will also do it.

ISAIAH 46:10b, 11b

The Lord is not slack concerning His promise, as some count slackness, but is longsuffering toward us, not willing that any should perish but that all should come to repentance.

2 PETER 3:9

As for God, His way is perfect; the word of the LORD is proven; He is a shield to all who trust in Him.

PSALM 18:30

The LORD's hand is not shortened, that it cannot save; nor His ear heavy, that it cannot hear.

ISAIAH 59:1

Beloved, do not think it strange concerning the fiery trial which is to try you, as though some strange thing happened to you; but rejoice to the extent that you partake of Christ's sufferings, that when His glory is revealed, you may also be glad with exceeding joy.

1 PETER 4:12, 13

For as the rain comes down, and the snow from heaven,
And do not return there,
But water the earth,
And make it bring forth and bud,
That it may give seed to the sower
And bread to the eater,
So shall My word be that goes forth from My mouth;
It shall not return to Me void,
But it shall accomplish what I please,
And it shall prosper in the thing for which I sent it.

ISAIAH 55:10, 11

WHAT TO
DO WHEN . . .

WHAT TO DO WHEN YOU NEED CONFIDENCE

I can do all things through Christ who strengthens me.

PHILIPPIANS 4:13

So we may boldly say: "The LORD is my helper; I will not fear. What can man do to me?"

HEBREWS 13:6

Do not cast away your confidence, which has great reward.

For you have need of endurance, so that after you have done the will of God, you may receive the promise.

HEBREWS 10:35, 36

Being confident of this very thing, that He who has begun a good work in you will complete it until the day of Jesus Christ.

PHILIPPIANS 1:6

In all these things we are more than conquerors through Him who loved us.

ROMANS 8:37

The LORD God is my strength; He will make my feet like deer's feet, and He will make me walk on my high hills.

HABAKKUK 3:19

Now this is the confidence that we have in Him, that if we ask anything according to His will, He hears us.

And if we know that He hears us, whatever we ask, we know that we have the petitions that we have asked of Him.

1 JOHN 5:14, 15

Those who wait on the LORD
Shall renew their strength;
They shall mount up with wings like eagles,
They shall run and not be weary,
They shall walk and not faint.

ISAIAH 40:31

When you pass through the waters, I will be with you;
And through the rivers, they shall not overflow you.
When you walk through the fire, you shall not be burned,
Nor shall the flame scorch you.

ISAIAH 43:2

So he answered and said to me:
"This is the word of the LORD to Zerubbabel:
'Not by might nor by power, but by My Spirit,'
Says the LORD of hosts."

ZECHARIAH 4:6

The LORD will be your confidence,
And will keep your foot from being caught.

PROVERBS 3:26

Therefore I rejoice that I have confidence in you in everything.

2 CORINTHIANS 7:16

In whom we have boldness and access with confidence through faith in Him.

EPHESIANS 3:12

Beloved, if our heart does not condemn us, we have confidence toward God.

1 JOHN 3:21

Most assuredly, I say to you, he who believes in Me, the works that I do he will do also; and greater works than these he will do, because I go to My Father.

JOHN 14:12

What to Do When You Have Troubles in Your Life

The LORD is good, a stronghold in the day of trouble;
and He knows those who trust in Him.

NAHUM 1:7

We are hard pressed on every side, yet not crushed;
we are perplexed, but not in despair; persecuted, but
not forsaken; struck down, but not destroyed.

2 CORINTHIANS 4:8, 9

Though I walk in the midst of trouble, You will revive
me;
You will stretch out Your hand
Against the wrath of my enemies,
And Your right hand will save me.

PSALM 138:7

For we do not have a High Priest who cannot sympathize with our weaknesses, but was in all points tempted
as we are, yet without sin. Let us therefore come boldly
to the throne of grace, that we may obtain mercy and
find grace to help in time of need.

HEBREWS 4:15, 16

Do not worry about tomorrow, for tomorrow will worry about its own things. Sufficient for the day is its own trouble.

MATTHEW 6:34

Let not your heart be troubled; you believe in God, believe also in Me.

JOHN 14:1

We know that all things work together for good to those who love God, to those who are the called according to His purpose.

ROMANS 8:28

I will be glad and rejoice in Your mercy, for You have considered my trouble; You have known my soul in adversities.

PSALM 31:7

I will lift up my eyes to the hills—
From whence comes my help?
My help comes from the LORD,
Who made heaven and earth.

PSALM 121:1, 2

Casting all your care upon Him, for He cares for you.

1 PETER 5:7

Blessed be the God and Father of our Lord Jesus Christ, the Father of mercies and God of all comfort, who comforts us in all our tribulation, that we may be able to comfort those who are in any trouble, with the comfort with which we ourselves are comforted by God.

2 CORINTHIANS 1:3, 4

Be anxious for nothing, but in everything by prayer and supplication, with thanksgiving, let your requests be made known to God; and the peace of God, which surpasses all understanding, will guard your hearts and minds through Christ Jesus.

PHILIPPIANS 4:6, 7

What to Do When You Have
Financial Troubles

I pray that you may prosper in all things and be in health, just as your soul prospers.

3 John 2

The young lions lack and suffer hunger; but those who seek the Lord shall not lack any good thing.

Psalm 34:10

I have been young, and now am old; yet I have not seen the righteous forsaken, nor his descendants begging bread.

Psalm 37:25

Do not worry, saying, "What shall we eat?" or "What shall we drink?" or "What shall we wear?"

For after all these things the Gentiles seek. For your heavenly Father knows that you need all these things.

But seek first the kingdom of God and His righteousness, and all these things shall be added to you.

Matthew 6:31–33

The LORD is my shepherd; I shall not want.

PSALM 23:1

The LORD will grant you plenty of goods, in the fruit of your body, in the increase of your livestock, and in the produce of your ground, in the land of which the LORD swore to your fathers to give you.

The LORD will open to you His good treasure, the heavens, to give the rain to your land in its season, and to bless all the work of your hand. You shall lend to many nations, but you shall not borrow.

And the LORD will make you the head and not the tail; you shall be above only, and not be beneath, if you heed the commandments of the LORD your God, which I command you today, and are careful to observe them.

DEUTERONOMY 28:11–13

My God shall supply all your need according to His riches in glory by Christ Jesus.

PHILIPPIANS 4:19

Heal the sick, cleanse the lepers, raise the dead, cast out demons. Freely you have received, freely give.

MATTHEW 10:8

Give, and it will be given to you: good measure, pressed down, shaken together, and running over will be put into your bosom. For with the same measure that you use, it will be measured back to you.

LUKE 6:38

On the first day of the week let each one of you lay something aside, storing up as he may prosper, that there be no collections when I come.

1 CORINTHIANS 16:2

But this I say: He who sows sparingly will also reap sparingly, and he who sows bountifully will also reap bountifully.

So let each one give as he purposes in his heart, not grudgingly or of necessity; for God loves a cheerful giver.

And God is able to make all grace abound toward you, that you, always having all sufficiency in all things, may have an abundance for every good work.

2 CORINTHIANS 9:6–8

WHAT TO DO WHEN YOU HAVE MARITAL PROBLEMS

Let all bitterness, wrath, anger, clamor, and evil speaking be put away from you, with all malice.

And be kind to one another, tenderhearted, forgiving one another, even as God in Christ forgave you.

EPHESIANS 4:31, 32

And the LORD God said, "It is not good that man should be alone; I will make him a helper comparable to him."

GENESIS 2:18

Therefore a man shall leave his father and mother and be joined to his wife, and they shall become one flesh.

GENESIS 2:24

And if it seems evil to you to serve the LORD, choose for yourselves this day whom you will serve, whether the gods which your fathers served that were on the other side of the River, or the gods of the Amorites, in whose land you dwell. But as for me and my house, we will serve the LORD.

JOSHUA 24:15

Wives, likewise, be submissive to your own husbands, that even if some do not obey the word, they, without a word, may be won by the conduct of their wives, when they observe your chaste conduct accompanied by fear.

Do not let your adornment be merely outward—arranging the hair, wearing gold, or putting on fine apparel—rather let it be the hidden person of the heart, with the incorruptible beauty of a gentle and quiet spirit, which is very precious in the sight of God.

For in this manner, in former times, the holy women who trusted in God also adorned themselves, being submissive to their own husbands, as Sarah obeyed Abraham, calling him lord, whose daughters you are if you do good and are not afraid with any terror.

Husbands, likewise, dwell with them with understanding, giving honor to the wife, as to the weaker vessel, and as being heirs together of the grace of life, that your prayers may not be hindered.

1 PETER 3:1–7

Love does no harm to a neighbor; therefore love is the fulfillment of the law.

ROMANS 13:10

All of you be of one mind, having compassion for one another; love as brothers, be tenderhearted, be courteous; not returning evil for evil or reviling for reviling, but on the contrary blessing, knowing that you were called to this, that you may inherit a blessing.

For "He who would love life and see good days, let him refrain his tongue from evil, and his lips from speaking deceit. Let him turn away from evil and do good; let him seek peace and pursue it."

1 PETER 3:8–11

I will behave wisely in a perfect way. Oh, when will You come to me? I will walk within my house with a perfect heart.

PSALM 101:2

Trust in the LORD with all your heart,
And lean not on your own understanding;
In all your ways acknowledge Him,
And He shall direct your paths.

PROVERBS 3:5, 6

Hatred stirs up strife, but love covers all sins.

PROVERBS 10:12

WHAT TO DO WHEN YOU ARE
DESERTED BY LOVED ONES

And those who know Your name will put their trust in You; for You, LORD, have not forsaken those who seek You.

PSALM 9:10

When my father and my mother forsake me, then the LORD will take care of me.

PSALM 27:10

For the LORD will not cast off His people, nor will He forsake His inheritance.

PSALM 94:14

Teaching them to observe all things that I have commanded you; and lo, I am with you always, even to the end of the age.

MATTHEW 28:20

The LORD your God is a merciful God, He will not forsake you nor destroy you, nor forget the covenant of your fathers which He swore to them.

DEUTERONOMY 4:31

Persecuted, but not forsaken; struck down, but not destroyed.

2 CORINTHIANS 4:9

Casting all your care upon Him, for He cares for you.

1 PETER 5:7

I have been young, and now am old; yet I have not seen the righteous forsaken, nor his descendants begging bread.

PSALM 37:25

Because he has set his love upon Me, therefore I will
    deliver him;
I will set him on high, because he has known My
    name.
He shall call upon Me, and I will answer him;
I will be with him in trouble;
I will deliver him and honor him.

PSALM 91:14, 15

The poor and needy seek water, but there is none,
Their tongues fail for thirst.
I, the LORD, will hear them;
I, the God of Israel, will not forsake them.

ISAIAH 41:17

Can a woman forget her nursing child,
And not have compassion on the son of her womb?
Surely they may forget,
Yet I will not forget you.
See, I have inscribed you on the palms of My hands;
Your walls are continually before Me.

ISAIAH 49:15, 16

Why are you cast down, O my soul?
And why are you disquieted within me?
Hope in God;
For I shall yet praise Him,
The help of my countenance and my God.

PSALM 43:5

Be strong and of good courage, do not fear nor be
afraid of them; for the LORD your God, He is the
One who goes with you. He will not leave you nor
forsake you.

DEUTERONOMY 31:6

WHAT TO DO WHEN YOU DON'T UNDERSTAND GOD'S WAYS

I will make an everlasting covenant with them, that I will not turn away from doing them good; but I will put My fear in their hearts so that they will not depart from Me.

JEREMIAH 32:40

Call to Me, and I will answer you, and show you great and mighty things, which you do not know.

JEREMIAH 33:3

What then shall we say to these things? If God is for us, who can be against us?

ROMANS 8:31

Who shall separate us from the love of Christ? Shall tribulation, or distress, or persecution, or famine, or nakedness, or peril, or sword?

As it is written: "For Your sake we are killed all day long; we are accounted as sheep for the slaughter."

Yet in all these things we are more than conquerors through Him who loved us.

ROMANS 8:35–37

No temptation has overtaken you except such as is common to man; but God is faithful, who will not allow you to be tempted beyond what you are able, but with the temptation will also make the way of escape, that you may be able to bear it.

1 CORINTHIANS 10:13

Many are the afflictions of the righteous, but the LORD delivers him out of them all.

PSALM 34:19

Cast your burden on the LORD, and He shall sustain you; He shall never permit the righteous to be moved.

PSALM 55:22

Fear not, for I am with you;
Be not dismayed, for I am your God.
I will strengthen you,
Yes, I will help you,
I will uphold you with My righteous right hand.

ISAIAH 41:10

We know that all things work together for good to those who love God, to those who are the called according to His purpose.

ROMANS 8:28

As for God, His way is perfect;
The word of the LORD is proven;
He is a shield to all who trust in Him.

PSALM 18:30

The LORD will perfect that which concerns me;
Your mercy, O LORD, endures forever;
Do not forsake the works of Your hands.

PSALM 138:8

Let us hold fast the confession of our hope without
wavering, for He who promised is faithful.

HEBREWS 10:23

"For My thoughts are not your thoughts,
Nor are your ways My ways," says the LORD.
"For as the heavens are higher than the earth,
So are My ways higher than your ways,
And My thoughts than your thoughts."

ISAIAH 55:8, 9

WHAT TO DO WHEN YOU ARE WAITING ON GOD

Wait on the LORD; be of good courage, and He shall strengthen your heart; wait, I say, on the LORD!

PSALM 27:14

For we have become partakers of Christ if we hold the beginning of our confidence steadfast to the end.

HEBREWS 3:14

Our soul waits for the LORD;
He is our help and our shield.

PSALM 33:20

My soul, wait silently for God alone,
For my expectation is from Him.

PSALM 62:5

Those who wait on the LORD
Shall renew their strength;
They shall mount up with wings like eagles,
They shall run and not be weary,
They shall walk and not faint.

ISAIAH 40:31

For the vision is yet for an appointed time;
But at the end it will speak, and it will not lie.
Though it tarries, wait for it;
Because it will surely come,
It will not tarry.

HABAKKUK 2:3

Let us hold fast the confession of our hope without wavering, for He who promised is faithful.

HEBREWS 10:23

I wait for the LORD, my soul waits,
And in His word I do hope.

PSALM 130:5

The eyes of all look expectantly to You,
And You give them their food in due season.
You open Your hand
And satisfy the desire of every living thing.

PSALM 145:15, 16

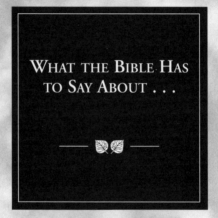

WHAT THE BIBLE HAS
TO SAY ABOUT . . .

WHAT THE BIBLE HAS TO SAY ABOUT FAITH

Whatever is born of God overcomes the world. And this is the victory that has overcome the world—our faith.

1 JOHN 5:4

Now faith is the substance of things hoped for, the evidence of things not seen.

HEBREWS 11:1

So Jesus answered and said to them, "Have faith in God.

"For assuredly, I say to you, whoever says to this mountain, 'Be removed and be cast into the sea,' and does not doubt in his heart, but believes that those things he says will be done, he will have whatever he says.

"Therefore I say to you, whatever things you ask when you pray, believe that you receive them, and you will have them."

MARK 11:22–24

But without faith it is impossible to please Him, for he who comes to God must believe that He is, and that He is a rewarder of those who diligently seek Him.

HEBREWS 11:6

Jesus said to him, "If you can believe, all things are possible to him who believes."

MARK 9:23

That the genuineness of your faith, being much more precious than gold that perishes, though it is tested by fire, may be found to praise, honor, and glory at the revelation of Jesus Christ, whom having not seen you love. Though now you do not see Him, yet believing, you rejoice with joy inexpressible and full of glory, receiving the end of your faith—the salvation of your souls.

1 PETER 1:7–9

So then faith comes by hearing, and hearing by the word of God.

ROMANS 10:17

A woman who had a flow of blood for twelve years came from behind and touched the hem of His garment.

For she said to herself, "If only I may touch His garment, I shall be made well."

But Jesus turned around, and when He saw her He said, "Be of good cheer, daughter; your faith has made you well." And the woman was made well from that hour.

MATTHEW 9:20–22

When He had come into the house, the blind men came to Him. And Jesus said to them, "Do you believe that I am able to do this?" They said to Him, "Yes, Lord."

Then He touched their eyes, saying, "According to your faith let it be to you."

MATTHEW 9:28, 29

Is anyone among you sick? Let him call for the elders of the church, and let them pray over him, anointing him with oil in the name of the Lord.

And the prayer of faith will save the sick, and the Lord will raise him up. And if he has committed sins, he will be forgiven.

JAMES 5:14, 15

What the Bible Has to Say About Love

Beloved, let us love one another, for love is of God; and everyone who loves is born of God and knows God.

He who does not love does not know God, for God is love.

1 John 4:7, 8

In this is love, not that we loved God, but that He loved us and sent His Son to be the propitiation for our sins.

Beloved, if God so loved us, we also ought to love one another.

No one has seen God at any time. If we love one another, God abides in us, and His love has been perfected in us.

1 John 4:10–12

As the Father loved Me, I also have loved you; abide in My love.

If you keep My commandments, you will abide in My love, just as I have kept My Father's commandments and abide in His love.

John 15:9, 10

Though I speak with the tongues of men and of angels, but have not love, I have become sounding brass or a clanging cymbal.

And though I have the gift of prophecy, and understand all mysteries and all knowledge, and though I have all faith, so that I could remove mountains, but have not love, I am nothing.

And though I bestow all my goods to feed the poor, and though I give my body to be burned, but have not love, it profits me nothing.

Love suffers long and is kind; love does not envy; love does not parade itself, is not puffed up; does not behave rudely, does not seek its own, is not provoked, thinks no evil; does not rejoice in iniquity, but rejoices in the truth; bears all things, believes all things, hopes all things, endures all things.

Love never fails. But whether there are prophecies, they will fail; whether there are tongues, they will cease; whether there is knowledge, it will vanish away.

And now abide faith, hope, love, these three; but the greatest of these is love.

1 CORINTHIANS 13:1–8, 13

The Father Himself loves you, because you have loved Me, and have believed that I came forth from God.

JOHN 16:27

He who has My commandments and keeps them, it is he who loves Me. And he who loves Me will be loved by My Father, and I will love him and manifest Myself to him.

JOHN 14:21

The LORD has appeared of old to me, saying:
"Yes, I have loved you with an everlasting love;
Therefore with lovingkindness I have drawn you."

JEREMIAH 31:3

God demonstrates His own love toward us, in that while we were still sinners, Christ died for us.

ROMANS 5:8

I am persuaded that neither death nor life, nor angels nor principalities nor powers, nor things present nor things to come, nor height nor depth, nor any other created thing, shall be able to separate us from the love of God which is in Christ Jesus our Lord.

ROMANS 8:38, 39

What the Bible Has to Say About Eternity

This is the testimony: that God has given us eternal life, and this life is in His Son.

1 John 5:11

God so loved the world that He gave His only begotten Son, that whoever believes in Him should not perish but have everlasting life.

John 3:16

Most assuredly, I say to you, he who hears My word and believes in Him who sent Me has everlasting life, and shall not come into judgment, but has passed from death into life.

John 5:24

Most assuredly, I say to you, he who believes in Me has everlasting life.

John 6:47

The poor shall eat and be satisfied; those who seek Him will praise the LORD. Let your heart live forever!

Psalm 22:26

I am the living bread which came down from heaven. If anyone eats of this bread, he will live forever; and the bread that I shall give is My flesh, which I shall give for the life of the world.

JOHN 6:51

We know that the Son of God has come and has given us an understanding, that we may know Him who is true; and we are in Him who is true, in His Son Jesus Christ. This is the true God and eternal life.

JOHN 5:20

Surely goodness and mercy shall follow me all the days of my life; and I will dwell in the house of the LORD forever.

PSALM 23:6

The LORD knows the days of the upright, and their inheritance shall be forever.

PSALM 37:18

Do not labor for the food which perishes, but for the food which endures to everlasting life, which the Son of Man will give you, because God the Father has set His seal on Him.

JOHN 6:27

God will redeem my soul from the power of the grave, for He shall receive me.

PSALM 49:15

When this corruptible has put on incorruption, and this mortal has put on immortality, then shall be brought to pass the saying that is written: "Death is swallowed up in victory. O Death, where is your sting? O Hades, where is your victory?"

1 CORINTHIANS 15:54, 55

Jesus said to her, "I am the resurrection and the life. He who believes in Me, though he may die, he shall live.

"And whoever lives and believes in Me shall never die. Do you believe this?"

JOHN 11:25, 26

My sheep hear My voice, and I know them, and they follow Me.

And I give them eternal life, and they shall never perish; neither shall anyone snatch them out of My hand.

JOHN 10:27, 28

What the Bible Has to Say About Praise

This people I have formed for Myself;
They shall declare My praise.

ISAIAH 43:21

You are a chosen generation, a royal priesthood, a holy nation, His own special people, that you may proclaim the praises of Him who called you out of darkness into His marvelous light.

1 PETER 2:9

Therefore by Him let us continually offer the sacrifice of praise to God, that is, the fruit of our lips, giving thanks to His name.

HEBREWS 13:15

Oh, clap your hands, all you peoples!
Shout to God with the voice of triumph!
Sing praises to God, sing praises!
Sing praises to our King, sing praises!
For God is the King of all the earth;
Sing praises with understanding.

PSALM 47:1, 6, 7

Praise the LORD!
For it is good to sing praises to our God;
For it is pleasant, and praise is beautiful.

PSALM 147:1

I will call upon the LORD, who is worthy to be praised;
so shall I be saved from my enemies.

2 SAMUEL 22:4

I will bless the LORD at all times; His praise shall continually be in my mouth.

PSALM 34:1

Great is the LORD, and greatly to be praised in the city of our God, in His holy mountain.

PSALM 48:1

Whoever offers praise glorifies Me; and to him who orders his conduct aright I will show the salvation of God.

PSALM 50:23

Oh, that men would give thanks to the LORD for His goodness, and for His wonderful works to the children of men!

PSALM 107:8

Because Your lovingkindness is better than life,
My lips shall praise You.
Thus I will bless You while I live;
I will lift up my hands in Your name.
My soul shall be satisfied as with marrow and fatness,
And my mouth shall praise You with joyful lips.

PSALM 63:3–5

Let my mouth be filled with Your praise
And with Your glory all the day.
But I will hope continually,
And will praise You yet more and more.

PSALM 71:8, 14

It is good to give thanks to the LORD,
And to sing praises to Your name, O Most High.

PSALM 92:1

The LORD is great and greatly to be praised;
He is to be feared above all gods.

PSALM 96:4

At midnight Paul and Silas were praying and singing hymns to God, and the prisoners were listening to them.

ACTS 16:25

What the Bible Has to Say About Serving God

You shall walk after the LORD your God and fear Him, and keep His commandments and obey His voice; you shall serve Him and hold fast to Him.

DEUTERONOMY 13:4

Then Jesus said to him, "Away with you, Satan! For it is written, 'You shall worship the LORD your God, and Him only you shall serve.'"

MATTHEW 4:10

No one can serve two masters; for either he will hate the one and love the other, or else he will be loyal to the one and despise the other. You cannot serve God and mammon.

MATTHEW 6:24

Take careful heed to do the commandment and the law which Moses the servant of the LORD commanded you, to love the LORD your God, to walk in all His ways, to keep His commandments, to hold fast to Him, and to serve Him with all your heart and with all your soul.

JOSHUA 22:5

It shall be that if you earnestly obey My command-ments which I command you today, to love the LORD your God and serve Him with all your heart and with all your soul, then I will give you the rain for your land in its season, the early rain and the latter rain, that you may gather in your grain, your new wine, and your oil.

And I will send grass in your fields for your live-stock, that you may eat and be filled.

DEUTERONOMY 11:13–15

I beseech you therefore, brethren, by the mercies of God, that you present your bodies a living sacrifice, holy, acceptable to God, which is your reasonable service.

And do not be conformed to this world, but be transformed by the renewing of your mind, that you may prove what is that good and acceptable and per-fect will of God.

ROMANS 12:1, 2

And now, Israel, what does the LORD your God require of you, but to fear the LORD your God, to walk in all His ways and to love Him, to serve the LORD your God with all your heart and with all your soul.

DEUTERONOMY 10:12

Be kindly affectionate to one another with brotherly love, in honor giving preference to one another; not lagging in diligence, fervent in spirit, serving the Lord; . . . distributing to the needs of the saints, given to hospitality.

ROMANS 12:10, 11, 13

You shall serve the LORD your God, and He will bless your bread and your water. And I will take sickness away from the midst of you.

No one shall suffer miscarriage or be barren in your land; I will fulfill the number of your days.

EXODUS 23:25, 26

If it seems evil to you to serve the LORD, choose for yourselves this day whom you will serve, whether the gods which your fathers served that were on the other side of the River, or the gods of the Amorites, in whose land you dwell. But as for me and my house, we will serve the LORD.

JOSHUA 24:15

Serve the LORD with gladness;
Come before His presence with singing.

PSALM 100:2

WHAT THE BIBLE HAS TO SAY ABOUT OBEDIENCE

Behold, I set before you today a blessing and a curse: the blessing, if you obey the commandments of the LORD your God which I command you today; and the curse, if you do not obey the commandments of the LORD your God, but turn aside from the way which I command you today, to go after other gods which you have not known.

DEUTERONOMY 11:26–28

So Samuel said: "Has the LORD as great delight in burnt offerings and sacrifices, as in obeying the voice of the LORD? Behold, to obey is better than sacrifice, and to heed than the fat of rams."

1 SAMUEL 15:22

If you love Me, keep My commandments.

He who has My commandments and keeps them, it is he who loves Me. And he who loves Me will be loved by My Father, and I will love him and manifest Myself to him.

JOHN 14:15, 21

Oh, that you had heeded My commandments!
Then your peace would have been like a river,
   And your righteousness like the waves of the sea.

ISAIAH 48:18

But this is what I commanded them, saying, "Obey
My voice, and I will be your God, and you shall be
My people. And walk in all the ways that I have com-
manded you, that it may be well with you."

JEREMIAH 7:23

Now by this we know that we know Him, if we keep
His commandments.

He who says, "I know Him," and does not keep His
commandments, is a liar, and the truth is not in him.

But whoever keeps His word, truly the love of God
is perfected in him. By this we know that we are in
Him.

He who says he abides in Him ought himself also
to walk just as He walked.

1 JOHN 2:3–6

Peter and the other apostles answered and said: "We
ought to obey God rather than men."

ACTS 5:29

So if you walk in My ways, to keep My statutes and My commandments, as your father David walked, then I will lengthen your days.

1 KINGS 3:14

> Teach me to do Your will,
> For You are my God;
> Your Spirit is good.
> Lead me in the land of uprightness.

PSALM 143:10

And Moses called all Israel, and said to them: "Hear, O Israel, the statutes and judgments which I speak in your hearing today, that you may learn them and be careful to observe them.

"Therefore you shall be careful to do as the LORD your God has commanded you; you shall not turn aside to the right hand or to the left.

"You shall walk in all the ways which the LORD your God has commanded you, that you may live and that it may be well with you, and that you may prolong your days in the land which you shall possess."

DEUTERONOMY 5:1, 32, 33

What the Bible Has to Say About the Carnal Mind

To be carnally minded is death, but to be spiritually minded is life and peace.

Because the carnal mind is enmity against God; for it is not subject to the law of God, nor indeed can be.

So then, those who are in the flesh cannot please God.

ROMANS 8:6–8

He who sows to his flesh will of the flesh reap corruption, but he who sows to the Spirit will of the Spirit reap everlasting life.

GALATIANS 6:8

Adulterers and adulteresses! Do you not know that friendship with the world is enmity with God? Whoever therefore wants to be a friend of the world makes himself an enemy of God.

JAMES 4:4

There is a way that seems right to a man,
But its end is the way of death.

PROVERBS 14:12

Many walk, of whom I have told you often, and now tell you even weeping, that they are the enemies of the cross of Christ: whose end is destruction, whose god is their belly, and whose glory is in their shame—who set their mind on earthly things.

PHILIPPIANS 3:18, 19

No one engaged in warfare entangles himself with the affairs of this life, that he may please him who enlisted him as a soldier.

Flee also youthful lusts; but pursue righteousness, faith, love, peace with those who call on the Lord out of a pure heart.

2 TIMOTHY 2:4, 22

Let this mind be in you which was also in Christ Jesus.

PHILIPPIANS 2:5

Set your mind on things above, not on things on the earth.

COLOSSIANS 3:2

Beloved, I beg you as sojourners and pilgrims, abstain from fleshly lusts which war against the soul.

1 PETER 2:11

I beseech you therefore, brethren, by the mercies of God, that you present your bodies a living sacrifice, holy, acceptable to God, which is your reasonable service.

And do not be conformed to this world, but be transformed by the renewing of your mind, that you may prove what is that good and acceptable and perfect will of God.

ROMANS 12:1, 2

Do not love the world or the things in the world. If anyone loves the world, the love of the Father is not in him.

For all that is in the world—the lust of the flesh, the lust of the eyes, and the pride of life—is not of the Father but is of the world.

And the world is passing away, and the lust of it; but he who does the will of God abides forever.

1 JOHN 2:15–17

What the Bible Has to Say About the Grace of God

With great power the apostles gave witness to the resurrection of the Lord Jesus. And great grace was upon them all.

ACTS 4:33

And so find favor and high esteem
In the sight of God and man.

PROVERBS 3:4

The LORD has been mindful of us;
He will bless us;
He will bless the house of Israel;
He will bless the house of Aaron.
He will bless those who fear the LORD,
Both small and great.

PSALM 115:12, 13

For the LORD God is a sun and shield;
The LORD will give grace and glory;
No good thing will He withhold
From those who walk uprightly.

PSALM 84:11

The sons of foreigners shall build up your walls,
And their kings shall minister to you;
For in My wrath I struck you,
But in My favor I have had mercy on you.

ISAIAH 60:10

So the LORD said to Moses, "I will also do this thing that you have spoken; for you have found grace in My sight, and I know you by name."

EXODUS 33:17

You have granted me life and favor,
And Your care has preserved my spirit.

JOB 10:12

For You, O LORD, will bless the righteous;
With favor You will surround him as with a shield.

PSALM 5:12

LORD, by Your favor You have made my mountain stand strong; You hid Your face, and I was troubled.

PSALM 30:7

For whoever finds me finds life,
And obtains favor from the LORD;

PROVERBS 8:35

Blessings are on the head of the righteous,
But violence covers the mouth of the wicked.
The blessing of the LORD makes one rich,
And He adds no sorrow with it.
The fear of the wicked will come upon him,
And the desire of the righteous will be granted.

PROVERBS 10:6, 22, 24

Fools mock at sin,
But among the upright there is favor.

PROVERBS 14:9

All things are for your sakes, that grace, having spread through the many, may cause thanksgiving to abound to the glory of God.

2 CORINTHIANS 4:15

To the praise of the glory of His grace, by which He made us accepted in the Beloved.

EPHESIANS 1:6

Let us therefore come boldly to the throne of grace, that we may obtain mercy and find grace to help in time of need.

HEBREWS 4:16

What the Bible Has to Say About the Holy Spirit

Do you not know that your body is the temple of the Holy Spirit who is in you, whom you have from God, and you are not your own?

1 Corinthians 6:19

Now hope does not disappoint, because the love of God has been poured out in our hearts by the Holy Spirit who was given to us.

Romans 5:5

"He who believes in Me, as the Scripture has said, out of his heart will flow rivers of living water."

But this He spoke concerning the Spirit, whom those believing in Him would receive; for the Holy Spirit was not yet given, because Jesus was not yet glorified.

John 7:38, 39

If you then, being evil, know how to give good gifts to your children, how much more will your heavenly Father give the Holy Spirit to those who ask Him!

Luke 11:13

And being assembled together with them, He commanded them not to depart from Jerusalem, but to wait for the Promise of the Father, "which," He said, "you have heard from Me; for John truly baptized with water, but you shall be baptized with the Holy Spirit not many days from now.

"But you shall receive power when the Holy Spirit has come upon you; and you shall be witnesses to Me in Jerusalem, and in all Judea and Samaria, and to the end of the earth."

ACTS 1:4, 5, 8

Nevertheless I tell you the truth. It is to your advantage that I go away; for if I do not go away, the Helper will not come to you; but if I depart, I will send Him to you.

However, when He, the Spirit of truth, has come, He will guide you into all truth; for He will not speak on His own authority, but whatever He hears He will speak; and He will tell you things to come.

JOHN 16:7, 13

They were all filled with the Holy Spirit and began to speak with other tongues, as the Spirit gave them utterance.

ACTS 2:4

I indeed baptize you with water unto repentance, but He who is coming after me is mightier than I, whose sandals I am not worthy to carry. He will baptize you with the Holy Spirit and fire.

MATTHEW 3:11

And it shall come to pass afterward
That I will pour out My Spirit on all flesh;
Your sons and your daughters shall prophesy,
Your old men shall dream dreams,
Your young men shall see visions.

JOEL 2:28

I will pray the Father, and He will give you another Helper, that He may abide with you forever—the Spirit of truth, whom the world cannot receive, because it neither sees Him nor knows Him; but you know Him, for He dwells with you and will be in you.

JOHN 14:16, 17

Then Peter said to them, "Repent, and let every one of you be baptized in the name of Jesus Christ for the remission of sins; and you shall receive the gift of the Holy Spirit."

ACTS 2:38

WHAT THE BIBLE HAS TO SAY ABOUT GOD'S FAITHFULNESS

You have dealt well with Your servant,
O LORD, according to Your word.

PSALM 119:65

Behold, I am with you and will keep you wherever you go, and will bring you back to this land; for I will not leave you until I have done what I have spoken to you.

GENESIS 28:15

This is like the waters of Noah to Me;
For as I have sworn
That the waters of Noah would no longer cover the
    earth,
So have I sworn
That I would not be angry with you, nor rebuke you.
For the mountains shall depart
And the hills be removed,
But My kindness shall not depart from you,
Nor shall My covenant of peace be removed.

ISAIAH 54:9, 10

He who calls you is faithful, who also will do it.

1 THESSALONIANS 5:24

The rainbow shall be in the cloud, and I will look on it to remember the everlasting covenant between God and every living creature of all flesh that is on the earth.

GENESIS 9:16

Because the LORD loves you, and because He would keep the oath which He swore to your fathers, the LORD has brought you out with a mighty hand, and redeemed you from the house of bondage, from the hand of Pharaoh king of Egypt.

Therefore know that the LORD your God, He is God, the faithful God who keeps covenant and mercy for a thousand generations with those who love Him and keep His commandments.

DEUTERONOMY 7:8, 9

Behold, this day I am going the way of all the earth. And you know in all your hearts and in all your souls that not one thing has failed of all the good things which the LORD your God spoke concerning you. All have come to pass for you; not one word of them has failed.

JOSHUA 23:14

God is faithful, by whom you were called into the fellowship of His Son, Jesus Christ our Lord.

1 Corinthians 1:9

No temptation has overtaken you except such as is common to man; but God is faithful, who will not allow you to be tempted beyond what you are able, but with the temptation will also make the way of escape, that you may be able to bear it.

1 Corinthians 10:13

The Lord is not slack concerning His promise, as some count slackness, but is longsuffering toward us, not willing that any should perish but that all should come to repentance.

2 Peter 3:9

If we are faithless, He remains faithful; He cannot deny Himself.

Nevertheless the solid foundation of God stands, having this seal: "The Lord knows those who are His," and, "Let everyone who names the name of Christ depart from iniquity."

2 Timothy 2:13, 19

What the Bible Has to Say About the Church

That in the dispensation of the fullness of the times He might gather together in one all things in Christ, both which are in heaven and which are on earth—in Him.

And He put all things under His feet, and gave Him to be head over all things to the church, which is His body, the fullness of Him who fills all in all.

EPHESIANS 1:10, 22–23

He has delivered us from the power of darkness and conveyed us into the kingdom of the Son of His love.

And He is the head of the body, the church, who is the beginning, the firstborn from the dead, that in all things He may have the preeminence.

COLOSSIANS 1:13, 18

Blessed be the LORD, who has given rest to His people Israel, according to all that He promised. There has not failed one word of all His good promise, which He promised through His servant Moses.

1 KINGS 8:56

God's Promises

Your mercy, O LORD, is in the heavens;
Your faithfulness reaches to the clouds.

PSALM 36:5

I will sing of the mercies of the LORD forever;
With my mouth will I make known Your faithfulness
   to all generations.
For I have said, "Mercy shall be built up forever;
Your faithfulness You shall establish in the very
   heavens."
Nevertheless My lovingkindness I will not utterly
   take from him,
Nor allow My faithfulness to fail.
My covenant I will not break,
Nor alter the word that has gone out of My lips.

PSALM 89:1, 2, 33, 34

He will not allow your foot to be moved;
He who keeps you will not slumber.
Behold, He who keeps Israel
Shall neither slumber nor sleep.

PSALM 121:3, 4

He said to them, "But who do you say that I am?"

Simon Peter answered and said, "You are the Christ, the Son of the living God."

Jesus answered and said to him, "Blessed are you, Simon Bar-Jonah, for flesh and blood has not revealed this to you, but My Father who is in heaven.

"And I also say to you that you are Peter, and on this rock I will build My church, and the gates of Hades shall not prevail against it."

MATTHEW 16:15–18

Having been built on the foundation of the apostles and prophets, Jesus Christ Himself being the chief cornerstone, in whom the whole building, being fitted together, grows into a holy temple in the Lord, in whom you also are being built together for a dwelling place of God in the Spirit.

EPHESIANS 2:20–22

What the Bible Has to Say About Stewardship

Now concerning the collection for the saints, as I have given orders to the churches of Galatia, so you must do also: On the first day of the week let each one of you lay something aside, storing up as he may prosper, that there be no collections when I come.

1 Corinthians 16:1, 2

Give, and it will be given to you: good measure, pressed down, shaken together, and running over will be put into your bosom. For with the same measure that you use, it will be measured back to you.

Luke 6:38

But seek first the kingdom of God and His righteousness, and all these things shall be added to you.

Matthew 6:33

Whatever you do, do it heartily, as to the Lord and not to men, knowing that from the Lord you will receive the reward of the inheritance; for you serve the Lord Christ.

Colossians 3:23, 24

"Will a man rob God?
 Yet you have robbed Me!
'But you say,
 'In what way have we robbed You?'
 In tithes and offerings.
 You are cursed with a curse,
 For you have robbed Me,
 Even this whole nation.
 Bring all the tithes into the storehouse,
 That there may be food in My house,
 And try Me now in this,"
 Says the LORD of hosts,
"If I will not open for you the windows of heaven
 And pour out for you such blessing
 That there will not be room enough to receive it.
 And I will rebuke the devourer for your sakes,
 So that he will not destroy the fruit of your ground,
 Nor shall the vine fail to bear fruit for you in the field."

MALACHI 3:8–11

Lay up for yourselves treasures in heaven, where neither moth nor rust destroys and where thieves do not break in and steal.

For where your treasure is, there your heart will be also.

MATTHEW 6:20, 21

Heal the sick, cleanse the lepers, raise the dead, cast out demons. Freely you have received, freely give.

MATTHEW 10:8

But this I say: He who sows sparingly will also reap sparingly, and he who sows bountifully will also reap bountifully.

So let each one give as he purposes in his heart, not grudgingly or of necessity; for God loves a cheerful giver.

And God is able to make all grace abound toward you, that you, always having all sufficiency in all things, may have an abundance for every good work.

2 CORINTHIANS 9:6–8

Beloved, I pray that you may prosper in all things and be in health, just as your soul prospers.

3 JOHN 2

Everyone who has left houses or brothers or sisters or father or mother or wife or children or lands, for My name's sake, shall receive a hundredfold, and inherit eternal life.

MATTHEW 19:29

What the Bible Has to Say About Satan

Put on the whole armor of God, that you may be able to stand against the wiles of the devil.

For we do not wrestle against flesh and blood, but against principalities, against powers, against the rulers of the darkness of this age, against spiritual hosts of wickedness in the heavenly places.

Therefore take up the whole armor of God, that you may be able to withstand in the evil day, and having done all, to stand.

Stand therefore, having girded your waist with truth, having put on the breastplate of righteousness, and having shod your feet with the preparation of the gospel of peace; above all, taking the shield of faith with which you will be able to quench all the fiery darts of the wicked one.

And take the helmet of salvation, and the sword of the Spirit, which is the word of God; praying always with all prayer and supplication in the Spirit, being watchful to this end with all perseverance and supplication for all the saints.

EPHESIANS 6:11–18

Be sober, be vigilant; because your adversary the devil walks about like a roaring lion, seeking whom he may devour.

Resist him, steadfast in the faith, knowing that the same sufferings are experienced by your brotherhood in the world.

1 PETER 5:8, 9

Submit to God. Resist the devil and he will flee from you.

JAMES 4:7

We see Jesus, who was made a little lower than the angels, for the suffering of death crowned with glory and honor, that He, by the grace of God, might taste death for everyone.

Inasmuch then as the children have partaken of flesh and blood, He Himself likewise shared in the same, that through death He might destroy him who had the power of death, that is, the devil, and release those who through fear of death were all their lifetime subject to bondage.

HEBREWS 2:9, 14, 15

Then the seventy returned with joy, saying, "Lord, even the demons are subject to us in Your name."

And He said to them, "I saw Satan fall like lightning from heaven. Behold, I give you the authority to trample on serpents and scorpions, and over all the power of the enemy, and nothing shall by any means hurt you."

LUKE 10:17–19

These signs will follow those who believe: In My name they will cast out demons; they will speak with new tongues; they will take up serpents; and if they drink anything deadly, it will by no means hurt them; they will lay hands on the sick, and they will recover.

MARK 16:17, 18

If I cast out demons by the Spirit of God, surely the kingdom of God has come upon you.

Or how can one enter a strong man's house and plunder his goods, unless he first binds the strong man? And then he will plunder his house.

MATTHEW 12:28, 29

What the Bible Has to Say About the Return of Christ

But I do not want you to be ignorant, brethren, concerning those who have fallen asleep, lest you sorrow as others who have no hope.

For if we believe that Jesus died and rose again, even so God will bring with Him those who sleep in Jesus.

For this we say to you by the word of the Lord, that we who are alive and remain until the coming of the Lord will by no means precede those who are asleep.

For the Lord Himself will descend from heaven with a shout, with the voice of an archangel, and with the trumpet of God. And the dead in Christ will rise first.

Then we who are alive and remain shall be caught up together with them in the clouds to meet the Lord in the air. And thus we shall always be with the Lord.

Therefore comfort one another with these words.

1 Thessalonians 4:13–18

Looking for the blessed hope and glorious appearing of our great God and Savior Jesus Christ.

Titus 2:13

Who also said, "Men of Galilee, why do you stand gazing up into heaven? This same Jesus, who was taken up from you into heaven, will so come in like manner as you saw Him go into heaven."

ACTS 1:11

Beloved, now we are children of God; and it has not yet been revealed what we shall be, but we know that when He is revealed, we shall be like Him, for we shall see Him as He is.

And everyone who has this hope in Him purifies himself, just as He is pure.

1 JOHN 3:2, 3

And there will be signs in the sun, in the moon, and in the stars; and on the earth distress of nations, with perplexity, the sea and the waves roaring; men's hearts failing them from fear and the expectation of those things which are coming on the earth, for the powers of the heavens will be shaken.

Then they will see the Son of Man coming in a cloud with power and great glory.

Now when these things begin to happen, look up and lift up your heads, because your redemption draws near.

LUKE 21:25–28

There is laid up for me the crown of righteousness, which the Lord, the righteous Judge, will give to me on that Day, and not to me only but also to all who have loved His appearing.

2 TIMOTHY 4:8

So you also, when you see all these things, know that it is near—at the doors!

MATTHEW 24:33

Let not your heart be troubled; you believe in God, believe also in Me.

In My Father's house are many mansions; if it were not so, I would have told you. I go to prepare a place for you.

And if I go and prepare a place for you, I will come again and receive you to Myself; that where I am, there you may be also.

And where I go you know, and the way you know.

JOHN 14:1–4

WHAT THE BIBLE HAS TO SAY ABOUT THE UNSAVED

For all have sinned and fall short of the glory of God.

ROMANS 3:23

Therefore, just as through one man sin entered the world, and death through sin, and thus death spread to all men, because all sinned.

ROMANS 5:12

For the wages of sin is death, but the gift of God is eternal life in Christ Jesus our Lord.

ROMANS 6:23

For the wrath of God is revealed from heaven against all ungodliness and unrighteousness of men, who suppress the truth in unrighteousness, because what may be known of God is manifest in them, for God has shown it to them.

For since the creation of the world His invisible attributes are clearly seen, being understood by the things that are made, even His eternal power and Godhead, so that they are without excuse.

ROMANS 1:18–20

God demonstrates His own love toward us, in that while we were still sinners, Christ died for us.

ROMANS 5:8

The Lord is not slack concerning His promise, as some count slackness, but is longsuffering toward us, not willing that any should perish but that all should come to repentance.

2 PETER 3:9

For God did not send His Son into the world to condemn the world, but that the world through Him might be saved.

JOHN 3:17

I have not come to call the righteous, but sinners, to repentance.

LUKE 5:32

The Son of Man is come to seek and to save that which was lost.

LUKE 19:10

Jesus answered and said to him, "Most assuredly, I say to you, unless one is born again, he cannot see the kingdom of God."

JOHN 3:3

God so loved the world that He gave His only begotten Son, that whoever believes in Him should not perish but have everlasting life.

JOHN 3:16

And He said to them, "Go into all the world and preach the gospel to every creature.

"He who believes and is baptized will be saved; but he who does not believe will be condemned."

MARK 16:15, 16

The Spirit of the LORD is upon Me,
Because He has anointed Me
To preach the gospel to the poor;
He has sent Me to heal the brokenhearted,
To proclaim liberty to the captives
And recovery of sight to the blind,
To set at liberty those who are oppressed;
To proclaim the acceptable year of the LORD.

LUKE 4:18, 19

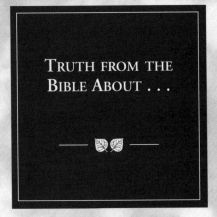

TRUTH FROM THE
BIBLE ABOUT . . .

TRUTH FROM THE BIBLE ABOUT FORGIVING OTHERS

If you forgive men their trespasses, your heavenly Father will also forgive you.

But if you do not forgive men their trespasses, neither will your Father forgive your trespasses.

MATTHEW 6:14, 15

Then Peter came to Him and said, "Lord, how often shall my brother sin against me, and I forgive him? Up to seven times?"

Jesus said to him, "I do not say to you, up to seven times, but up to seventy times seven."

MATTHEW 18:21, 22

Take heed to yourselves. If your brother sins against you, rebuke him; and if he repents, forgive him.

LUKE 17:3

Whenever you stand praying, if you have anything against anyone, forgive him, that your Father in heaven may also forgive you your trespasses.

MARK 11:25

Bearing with one another, and forgiving one another, if anyone has a complaint against another; even as Christ forgave you, so you also must do.

COLOSSIANS 3:13

Brethren, I do not count myself to have apprehended; but one thing I do, forgetting those things which are behind and reaching forward to those things which are ahead, I press toward the goal for the prize of the upward call of God in Christ Jesus.

PHILIPPIANS 3:13, 14

Do not remember the former things,
Nor consider the things of old.
Behold, I will do a new thing,
Now it shall spring forth;
Shall you not know it?
I will even make a road in the wilderness
And rivers in the desert.

ISAIAH 43:18, 19

For we know Him who said, "Vengeance is Mine, I will repay," says the Lord. And again, "The LORD will judge His people."

HEBREWS 10:30

Blessed are those who are persecuted for righteousness' sake, for theirs is the kingdom of heaven.

Blessed are you when they revile and persecute you, and say all kinds of evil against you falsely for My sake.

Rejoice and be exceedingly glad, for great is your reward in heaven, for so they persecuted the prophets who were before you.

MATTHEW 5:10–12

Truth from the Bible About Christian Fellowship

Walk in love, as Christ also has loved us and given Himself for us, an offering and a sacrifice to God for a sweet-smelling aroma.

Speaking to one another in psalms and hymns and spiritual songs, singing and making melody in your heart to the Lord . . .

For we are members of His body, of His flesh and of His bones.

Ephesians 5:2, 19, 30

Let the word of Christ dwell in you richly in all wisdom, teaching and admonishing one another in psalms and hymns and spiritual songs, singing with grace in your hearts to the Lord.

Colossians 3:16

That their hearts may be encouraged, being knit together in love, and attaining to all riches of the full assurance of understanding, to the knowledge of the mystery of God, both of the Father and of Christ.

Colossians 2:2

Then those who feared the LORD spoke to one another,
And the LORD listened and heard them;
So a book of remembrance was written before Him
For those who fear the LORD
And who meditate on His name.

MALACHI 3:16

That which we have seen and heard we declare to you, that you also may have fellowship with us; and truly our fellowship is with the Father and with His Son Jesus Christ.

But if we walk in the light as He is in the light, we have fellowship with one another, and the blood of Jesus Christ His Son cleanses us from all sin.

1 JOHN 1:3, 7

Now behold, two of them were traveling that same day to a village called Emmaus, which was seven miles from Jerusalem.

And they talked together of all these things which had happened.

So it was, while they conversed and reasoned, that Jesus Himself drew near and went with them.

LUKE 24:13–15

God's Promises

We took sweet counsel together,
And walked to the house of God in the throng.

PSALM 55:14

Now may the God of patience and comfort grant you
to be like-minded toward one another, according to
Christ Jesus, that you may with one mind and one
mouth glorify the God and Father of our Lord Jesus
Christ.

Therefore receive one another, just as Christ also
received us, to the glory of God.

ROMANS 15:5–7

Now I plead with you, brethren, by the name of our
Lord Jesus Christ, that you all speak the same thing,
and that there be no divisions among you, but that
you be perfectly joined together in the same mind
and in the same judgment.

1 CORINTHIANS 1:10

Bear one another's burdens, and so fulfill the law of
Christ.

Therefore, as we have opportunity, let us do good
to all, especially to those who are of the household of
faith.

GALATIANS 6:2, 10

TRUTH FROM THE BIBLE ABOUT YOUR RESPONSIBILITY

He said to them, "Go into all the world and preach the gospel to every creature."

MARK 16:15

You shall receive power when the Holy Spirit has come upon you; and you shall be witnesses to Me in Jerusalem, and in all Judea and Samaria, and to the end of the earth.

ACTS 1:8

You are the salt of the earth; but if the salt loses its flavor, how shall it be seasoned? It is then good for nothing but to be thrown out and trampled underfoot by men.

You are the light of the world. A city that is set on a hill cannot be hidden.

Nor do they light a lamp and put it under a basket, but on a lampstand, and it gives light to all who are in the house.

Let your light so shine before men, that they may see your good works and glorify your Father in heaven.

MATTHEW 5:13–16

I was hungry and you gave Me food; I was thirsty and you gave Me drink; I was a stranger and you took Me in; I was naked and you clothed Me; I was sick and you visited Me; I was in prison and you came to Me.

Then the righteous will answer Him, saying, "Lord, when did we see You hungry and feed You, or thirsty and give You drink?

"When did we see You a stranger and take You in, or naked and clothe You?

"Or when did we see You sick, or in prison, and come to You?"

And the King will answer and say to them, "Assuredly, I say to you, inasmuch as you did it to one of the least of these My brethren, you did it to Me."

MATTHEW 25:35–40

And whoever gives one of these little ones only a cup of cold water in the name of a disciple, assuredly, I say to you, he shall by no means lose his reward.

MATTHEW 10:42

God is not unjust to forget your work and labor of love which you have shown toward His name, in that you have ministered to the saints, and do minister.

HEBREWS 6:10

Pure and undefiled religion before God and the Father is this: to visit orphans and widows in their trouble, and to keep oneself unspotted from the world.

JAMES 1:27

If a brother or sister is naked and destitute of daily food, and one of you says to them, "Depart in peace, be warmed and filled," but you do not give them the things which are needed for the body, what does it profit?

Thus also faith by itself, if it does not have works, is dead.

JAMES 2:15–17

So the people asked him, saying, "What shall we do then?"

He answered and said to them, "He who has two tunics, let him give to him who has none; and he who has food, let him do likewise."

LUKE 3:10, 11

TRUTH FROM THE BIBLE ABOUT SPEAKING GOD'S WORD

Assuredly, I say to you, whoever says to this mountain, "Be removed and be cast into the sea," and does not doubt in his heart, but believes that those things he says will be done, he will have whatever he says.

MARK 11:23

So the Lord said, "If you have faith as a mustard seed, you can say to this mulberry tree, 'Be pulled up by the roots and be planted in the sea,' and it would obey you."

LUKE 17:6

Then He arose and rebuked the wind, and said to the sea, "Peace, be still!" And the wind ceased and there was a great calm.

MARK 4:39

Bless the LORD, you His angels, who excel in strength, who do His word, heeding the voice of His word.

PSALM 103:20

I have not spoken on My own authority; but the Father who sent Me gave Me a command, what I should say and what I should speak.

And I know that His command is everlasting life. Therefore, whatever I speak, just as the Father has told Me, so I speak.

JOHN 12:49, 50

I will raise up for them a Prophet like you from among their brethren, and will put My words in His mouth, and He shall speak to them all that I command Him.

DEUTERONOMY 18:18

The wise in heart will be called prudent,
And sweetness of the lips increases learning.
The heart of the wise teaches his mouth,
And adds learning to his lips.
Pleasant words are like a honeycomb,
Sweetness to the soul and health to the bones.
An ungodly man digs up evil,
And it is on his lips like a burning fire.
He winks his eye to devise perverse things;
He purses his lips and brings about evil.

PROVERBS 16:21, 23, 24, 27, 30

Brood of vipers! How can you, being evil, speak good things? For out of the abundance of the heart the mouth speaks.

But I say to you that for every idle word men may speak, they will give account of it in the day of judgment.

For by your words you will be justified, and by your words you will be condemned.

MATTHEW 12:34, 36, 37

If anyone among you thinks he is religious, and does not bridle his tongue but deceives his own heart, this one's religion is useless.

JAMES 1:26

Truth from the Bible About Finding the Will of God

If any of you lacks wisdom, let him ask of God, who gives to all liberally and without reproach, and it will be given to him.

JAMES 1:5

I will instruct you and teach you in the way you
    should go;
I will guide you with My eye.

PSALM 32:8

Your word is a lamp to my feet and a light to my path.

PSALM 119:105

When you roam, they will lead you;
When you sleep, they will keep you;
And when you awake, they will speak with you.
For the commandment is a lamp,
And the law a light;
Reproofs of instruction are the way of life.

PROVERBS 6:22, 23

Thus says the LORD, your Redeemer, the Holy One of Israel: "I am the LORD your God, Who teaches you to profit, Who leads you by the way you should go."

ISAIAH 48:17

Your ears shall hear a word behind you, saying,
"This is the way, walk in it,"
Whenever you turn to the right hand
Or whenever you turn to the left.

ISAIAH 30:21

The steps of a good man are ordered by the LORD,
And He delights in his way.

PSALM 37:23

For this is God, our God forever and ever;
He will be our guide even to death.

PSALM 48:14

Commit your works to the LORD,
And your thoughts will be established.

PROVERBS 16:3

You are my rock and my fortress;
Therefore, for Your name's sake,
Lead me and guide me.

PSALM 31:3

Trust in the LORD with all your heart,
And lean not on your own understanding;
In all your ways acknowledge Him,
And He shall direct your paths.

PROVERBS 3:5, 6

The LORD will guide you continually,
And satisfy your soul in drought,
And strengthen your bones;
You shall be like a watered garden,
And like a spring of water, whose waters do not fail.

ISAIAH 58:11

When He, the Spirit of truth, has come, He will guide
you into all truth; for He will not speak on His own
authority, but whatever He hears He will speak; and
He will tell you things to come.

JOHN 16:13

TRUTH FROM THE BIBLE ABOUT ANSWERED PRAYER

It shall come to pass that before they call, I will answer; and while they are still speaking, I will hear.

ISAIAH 65:24

Ask, and it will be given to you; seek, and you will find; knock, and it will be opened to you.

For everyone who asks receives, and he who seeks finds, and to him who knocks it will be opened.

MATTHEW 7:7, 8

And whatever things you ask in prayer, believing, you will receive.

MATTHEW 21:22

I say to you that if two of you agree on earth concerning anything that they ask, it will be done for them by My Father in heaven.

For where two or three are gathered together in My name, I am there in the midst of them.

MATTHEW 18:19, 20

And whatever you ask in My name, that I will do, that the Father may be glorified in the Son.

JOHN 14:13

If you abide in Me, and My words abide in you, you will ask what you desire, and it shall be done for you.

JOHN 15:7

And in that day you will ask Me nothing. Most assuredly, I say to you, whatever you ask the Father in My name He will give you.

JOHN 16:23

Let us therefore come boldly to the throne of grace, that we may obtain mercy and find grace to help in time of need.

HEBREWS 4:16

Delight yourself also in the LORD, and He shall give you the desires of your heart.

PSALM 37:4

He shall call upon Me, and I will answer him; I will be with him in trouble; I will deliver him and honor him.

PSALM 91:15

The LORD is near to all who call upon Him,
To all who call upon Him in truth.
He will fulfill the desire of those who fear Him;
He also will hear their cry and save them.

PSALM 145:18, 19

The LORD is far from the wicked,
But He hears the prayer of the righteous.

PROVERBS 15:29

Call to Me, and I will answer you, and show you great
and mighty things, which you do not know.

JEREMIAH 33:3

But you, when you pray, go into your room, and
when you have shut your door, pray to your Father
who is in the secret place; and your Father who sees
in secret will reward you openly.

MATTHEW 6:6

Whatever we ask we receive from Him, because we
keep His commandments and do those things that
are pleasing in His sight.

1 JOHN 3:22

TRUTH FROM THE BIBLE ABOUT UNSAVED LOVED ONES

Cast your burden on the LORD, and He shall sustain you; He shall never permit the righteous to be moved.

PSALM 55:22

Keep justice, and do righteousness, for My salvation is about to come, and My righteousness to be revealed.

ISAIAH 56:1

Nevertheless I tell you the truth. It is to your advantage that I go away; for if I do not go away, the Helper will not come to you; but if I depart, I will send Him to you.

And when He has come, He will convict the world of sin, and of righteousness, and of judgment.

JOHN 16:7, 8

I will pour water on him who is thirsty,
And floods on the dry ground;
I will pour My Spirit on your descendants,
And My blessing on your offspring.

ISAIAH 44:3

Who will tell you words by which you and all your household will be saved.

ACTS 11:14

So they said, "Believe on the Lord Jesus Christ, and you will be saved, you and your household."

ACTS 16:31

Even so it is not the will of your Father who is in heaven that one of these little ones should perish.

MATTHEW 18:14

Who among you fears the LORD?
Who obeys the voice of His Servant?
Who walks in darkness
And has no light?
Let him trust in the name of the LORD
And rely upon his God.

ISAIAH 50:10

The Lord is not slack concerning His promise, as some count slackness, but is longsuffering toward us, not willing that any should perish but that all should come to repentance.

2 PETER 3:9

TRUTH FROM THE BIBLE
ABOUT MARRIAGE

And the LORD God said, "It is not good that man should be alone; I will make him a helper comparable to him."

Therefore a man shall leave his father and mother and be joined to his wife, and they shall become one flesh.

GENESIS 2:18, 24

He who finds a wife finds a good thing,
And obtains favor from the LORD.

PROVERBS 18:22

Take wives and beget sons and daughters; and take wives for your sons and give your daughters to husbands, so that they may bear sons and daughters— that you may be increased there, and not diminished.

JEREMIAH 29:6

Marriage is honorable among all, and the bed undefiled; but fornicators and adulterers God will judge.

HEBREWS 13:4

Nevertheless, because of sexual immorality, let each man have his own wife, and let each woman have her own husband.

Let the husband render to his wife the affection due her, and likewise also the wife to her husband.

The wife does not have authority over her own body, but the husband does. And likewise the husband does not have authority over his own body, but the wife does.

1 CORINTHIANS 7:2–4

Therefore I desire that the younger widows marry, bear children, manage the house, give no opportunity to the adversary to speak reproachfully.

1 TIMOTHY 5:14

Wives, likewise, be submissive to your own husbands, that even if some do not obey the word, they, without a word, may be won by the conduct of their wives.

1 PETER 3:1

Wives, submit to your own husbands, as to the Lord.

For the husband is head of the wife, as also Christ is head of the church; and He is the Savior of the body.

Therefore, just as the church is subject to Christ, so let the wives be to their own husbands in everything.

Husbands, love your wives, just as Christ also loved the church and gave Himself for her, that He might sanctify and cleanse her with the washing of water by the word, that He might present her to Himself a glorious church, not having spot or wrinkle or any such thing, but that she should be holy and without blemish.

So husbands ought to love their own wives as their own bodies; he who loves his wife loves himself.

For no one ever hated his own flesh, but nourishes and cherishes it, just as the Lord does the church. For we are members of His body, of His flesh and of His bones.

EPHESIANS 5:22–31

TRUTH FROM THE BIBLE
ABOUT DIVORCE

The Pharisees also came to Him, testing Him, and saying to Him, "Is it lawful for a man to divorce his wife for just any reason?"

And He answered and said to them, "Have you not read that He who made them at the beginning 'made them male and female, . . . for this reason a man shall leave his father and mother and be joined to his wife, and the two shall become one flesh'? So then, they are no longer two but one flesh. Therefore what God has joined together, let not man separate."

They said to Him, "Why then did Moses command to give a certificate of divorce, and to put her away?"

He said to them, "Moses, because of the hardness of your hearts, permitted you to divorce your wives, but from the beginning it was not so. And I say to you, whoever divorces his wife, except for sexual immorality, and marries another, commits adultery; and whoever marries her who is divorced commits adultery."

MATTHEW 19:3–9

Now to the married I command, yet not I but the Lord: A wife is not to depart from her husband.

But even if she does depart, let her remain unmarried or be reconciled to her husband. And a husband is not to divorce his wife.

But to the rest I, not the Lord, say: If any brother has a wife who does not believe, and she is willing to live with him, let him not divorce her.

And a woman who has a husband who does not believe, if he is willing to live with her, let her not divorce him.

For the unbelieving husband is sanctified by the wife, and the unbelieving wife is sanctified by the husband; otherwise your children would be unclean, but now they are holy.

But if the unbeliever departs, let him depart; a brother or a sister is not under bondage in such cases. But God has called us to peace.

For how do you know, O wife, whether you will save your husband? Or how do you know, O husband, whether you will save your wife?

But as God has distributed to each one, as the Lord has called each one, so let him walk. And so I ordain in all the churches.

1 CORINTHIANS 7:10–17

Furthermore it has been said, "Whoever divorces his wife, let him give her a certificate of divorce."

But I say to you that whoever divorces his wife for any reason except sexual immorality causes her to commit adultery; and whoever marries a woman who is divorced commits adultery.

MATTHEW 5:31, 32

Whoever divorces his wife and marries another commits adultery; and whoever marries her who is divorced from her husband commits adultery.

LUKE 16:18

"They say, 'If a man divorces his wife,
    And she goes from him
    And becomes another man's,
    May he return to her again?'
    Would not that land be greatly polluted?
    But you have played the harlot with many lovers;
    Yet return to Me," says the LORD.

JEREMIAH 3:1

TRUTH FROM THE BIBLE ABOUT YOUR FAMILY

So they said, "Believe on the Lord Jesus Christ, and you will be saved, you and your household."

ACTS 16:31

And if it seems evil to you to serve the LORD, choose for yourselves this day whom you will serve, whether the gods which your fathers served that were on the other side of the River, or the gods of the Amorites, in whose land you dwell. But as for me and my house, we will serve the LORD.

JOSHUA 24:15

Let all bitterness, wrath, anger, clamor, and evil speaking be put away from you, with all malice.

And be kind to one another, tenderhearted, forgiving one another, even as God in Christ forgave you.

EPHESIANS 4:31, 32

Train up a child in the way he should go,
And when he is old he will not depart from it.

PROVERBS 22:6

These words which I command you today shall be in your heart.

You shall teach them diligently to your children, and shall talk of them when you sit in your house, when you walk by the way, when you lie down, and when you rise up.

You shall bind them as a sign on your hand, and they shall be as frontlets between your eyes.

You shall write them on the doorposts of your house and on your gates.

DEUTERONOMY 6:6–9

And he will turn
The hearts of the fathers to the children,
And the hearts of the children to their fathers,
Lest I come and strike the earth with a curse.

MALACHI 4:6

Children's children are the crown of old men,
And the glory of children is their father.

PROVERBS 17:6

Correct your son, and he will give you rest;
Yes, he will give delight to your soul.

PROVERBS 29:17

You, fathers, do not provoke your children to wrath, but bring them up in the training and admonition of the Lord.

EPHESIANS 6:4

A good man leaves an inheritance to his children's children, but the wealth of the sinner is stored up for the righteous.

PROVERBS 13:22

Blessed is every one who fears the LORD,
Who walks in His ways.
When you eat the labor of your hands,
You shall be happy, and it shall be well with you.
Your wife shall be like a fruitful vine
In the very heart of your house,
Your children like olive plants
All around your table.
Behold, thus shall the man be blessed
Who fears the LORD.

PSALM 128:1–4

The father of the righteous will greatly rejoice,
And he who begets a wise child will delight in him.

PROVERBS 23:24

TRUTH FROM THE BIBLE
ABOUT WIVES

Wives, likewise, be submissive to your own husbands, that even if some do not obey the word, they, without a word, may be won by the conduct of their wives, when they observe your chaste conduct accompanied by fear.

Do not let your adornment be merely outward—arranging the hair, wearing gold, or putting on fine apparel—rather let it be the hidden person of the heart, with the incorruptible beauty of a gentle and quiet spirit, which is very precious in the sight of God.

For in this manner, in former times, the holy women who trusted in God also adorned themselves, being submissive to their own husbands, as Sarah obeyed Abraham, calling him lord, whose daughters you are if you do good and are not afraid with any terror.

1 PETER 3:1–6

Wives, submit to your own husbands, as is fitting in the Lord.

COLOSSIANS 3:18

He who finds a wife finds a good thing,
And obtains favor from the LORD.

PROVERBS 18:22

Live joyfully with the wife whom you love all the days of your vain life which He has given you under the sun, all your days of vanity; for that is your portion in life, and in the labor which you perform under the sun.

ECCLESIASTES 9:9

Let the husband render to his wife the affection due her, and likewise also the wife to her husband.

1 CORINTHIANS 7:3

Let your fountain be blessed,
And rejoice with the wife of your youth.
As a loving deer and a graceful doe,
Let her breasts satisfy you at all times;
And always be enraptured with her love.

PROVERBS 5:18, 19

An excellent wife is the crown of her husband, but she who causes shame is like rottenness in his bones.

PROVERBS 12:4

The wise woman builds her house,
But the foolish pulls it down with her hands.

PROVERBS 14:1

Houses and riches are an inheritance from fathers,
But a prudent wife is from the LORD.

PROVERBS 19:14

Your wife shall be like a fruitful vine
In the very heart of your house,
Your children like olive plants
All around your table.

PSALM 128:3

TRUTH FROM THE BIBLE
ABOUT WIDOWS

Pure and undefiled religion before God and the Father is this: to visit orphans and widows in their trouble, and to keep oneself unspotted from the world.

JAMES 1:27

The blessing of a perishing man came upon me,
And I caused the widow's heart to sing for joy.

JOB 29:13

He administers justice for the fatherless and the widow, and loves the stranger, giving him food and clothing.

DEUTERONOMY 10:18

The LORD will destroy the house of the proud,
But He will establish the boundary of the widow.

PROVERBS 15:25

The LORD watches over the strangers;
He relieves the fatherless and widow;
But the way of the wicked He turns upside down.

PSALM 146:9

For your Maker is your husband,
The LORD of hosts is His name;
And your Redeemer is the Holy One of Israel;
He is called the God of the whole earth.

ISAIAH 54:5

A wife is bound by law as long as her husband lives;
but if her husband dies, she is at liberty to be married
to whom she wishes, only in the Lord.

But she is happier if she remains as she is, according to my judgment—and I think I also have the
Spirit of God.

1 CORINTHIANS 7:39, 40

I will not leave you orphans; I will come to you.

JOHN 14:18

A father of the fatherless, a defender of widows,
Is God in His holy habitation.

PSALM 68:5

He heals the brokenhearted
And binds up their wounds.

PSALM 147:3

Cursed is the one who perverts the justice due the stranger, the fatherless, and widow.

DEUTERONOMY 27:19

Therefore by Him let us continually offer the sacrifice of praise to God, that is, the fruit of our lips, giving thanks to His name.

HEBREWS 13:15

Lo, I am with you always, even to the end of the age.

MATTHEW 28:20

Therefore you now have sorrow; but I will see you again and your heart will rejoice, and your joy no one will take from you.

JOHN 16:22

TRUTH FROM THE BIBLE
ABOUT SINGLES

I will betroth you to Me forever;
Yes, I will betroth you to Me
In righteousness and justice,
In lovingkindness and mercy.

HOSEA 2:19

But I say to the unmarried and to the widows: It is good for them if they remain even as I am.

1 CORINTHIANS 7:8

But as God has distributed to each one, as the Lord has called each one, so let him walk. And so I ordain in all the churches.

Are you bound to a wife? Do not seek to be loosed. Are you loosed from a wife? Do not seek a wife.

But even if you do marry, you have not sinned; and if a virgin marries, she has not sinned. Nevertheless such will have trouble in the flesh, but I would spare you.

1 CORINTHIANS 7:17, 27, 28

Delight yourself also in the LORD,
And He shall give you the desires of your heart.

PSALM 37:4

But I want you to be without care. He who is unmarried cares for the things of the Lord—how he may please the Lord.

But he who is married cares about the things of the world—how he may please his wife.

And this I say for your own profit, not that I may put a leash on you, but for what is proper, and that you may serve the Lord without distraction.

1 CORINTHIANS 7:32, 33, 35

Nevertheless he who stands steadfast in his heart, having no necessity, but has power over his own will, and has so determined in his heart that he will keep his virgin, does well.

1 CORINTHIANS 7:37

Marriage is honorable among all, and the bed undefiled; but fornicators and adulterers God will judge.

HEBREWS 13:4

Trust in the LORD with all your heart, and lean not on your own understanding; in all your ways acknowledge Him, and He shall direct your paths.

PROVERBS 3:5, 6

Therefore, my brethren, you also have become dead to the law through the body of Christ, that you may be married to another—to Him who was raised from the dead, that we should bear fruit to God.

ROMANS 7:4

But let each one examine his own work, and then he will have rejoicing in himself alone, and not in another.

GALATIANS 6:4

To knowledge self-control, to self-control perseverance, to perseverance godliness, to godliness brotherly kindness, and to brotherly kindness love.

For if these things are yours and abound, you will be neither barren nor unfruitful in the knowledge of our Lord Jesus Christ.

2 PETER 1:6–8

TRUTH FROM THE BIBLE ABOUT THE ELDERLY

Even to your old age, I am He,
And even to gray hairs I will carry you!
I have made, and I will bear;
Even I will carry, and will deliver you.

ISAIAH 46:4

O God, You have taught me from my youth;
And to this day I declare Your wondrous works.
Now also when I am old and grayheaded,
O God, do not forsake me,
Until I declare Your strength to this generation,
Your power to everyone who is to come.

PSALM 71:17, 18

The silver-haired head is a crown of glory,
If it is found in the way of righteousness.

PROVERBS 16:31

The glory of young men is their strength,
And the splendor of old men is their gray head.

PROVERBS 20:29

I have been young, and now am old; yet I have not seen the righteous forsaken, nor his descendants begging bread.

PSALM 37:25

With long life I will satisfy him, and show him My salvation.

PSALM 91:16

For You, LORD, have made me glad through Your work; I will triumph in the works of Your hands.

PSALM 92:4

For length of days and long life and peace they will add to you.

PROVERBS 3:2

Let your conduct be without covetousness; be content with such things as you have. For He Himself has said, "I will never leave you nor forsake you."

HEBREWS 13:5

Yea, though I walk through the valley
   of the shadow of death,
I will fear no evil;
For You are with me;
Your rod and Your staff, they comfort me.

PSALM 23:4

Why are you cast down, O my soul?
And why are you disquieted within me?
Hope in God, for I shall yet praise Him
For the help of His countenance.

PSALM 42:5

For since the beginning of the world
Men have not heard nor perceived by the ear,
Nor has the eye seen any God besides You,
Who acts for the one who waits for Him.

ISAIAH 64:4

Surely goodness and mercy shall follow me all the
days of my life; and I will dwell in the house of the
LORD Forever.

PSALM 23:6

WHAT YOU CAN
DO TO . . .

What You Can Do to
Grow Spiritually

Who are kept by the power of God through faith for salvation ready to be revealed in the last time.

In this you greatly rejoice, though now for a little while, if need be, you have been grieved by various trials, that the genuineness of your faith, being much more precious than gold that perishes, though it is tested by fire, may be found to praise, honor, and glory at the revelation of Jesus Christ, whom having not seen you love. Though now you do not see Him, yet believing, you rejoice with joy inexpressible and full of glory.

1 Peter 1:5–8

Grow in the grace and knowledge of our Lord and Savior Jesus Christ. To Him be the glory both now and forever. Amen.

2 Peter 3:18

As newborn babes, desire the pure milk of the word, that you may grow thereby, if indeed you have tasted that the Lord is gracious.

1 Peter 2:2, 3

For this reason I bow my knees to the Father of our Lord Jesus Christ, from whom the whole family in heaven and earth is named, that He would grant you, according to the riches of His glory, to be strengthened with might through His Spirit in the inner man, that Christ may dwell in your hearts through faith; that you, being rooted and grounded in love, may be able to comprehend with all the saints what is the width and length and depth and height—to know the love of Christ which passes knowledge; that you may be filled with all the fullness of God.

EPHESIANS 3:14–19

For this reason we also, since the day we heard it, do not cease to pray for you, and to ask that you may be filled with the knowledge of His will in all wisdom and spiritual understanding; that you may walk worthy of the Lord, fully pleasing Him, being fruitful in every good work and increasing in the knowledge of God; strengthened with all might, according to His glorious power, for all patience and longsuffering with joy.

COLOSSIANS 1:9–11

Meditate on these things; give yourself entirely to them, that your progress may be evident to all.

1 TIMOTHY 4:15

Therefore, leaving the discussion of the elementary principles of Christ, let us go on to perfection, not laying again the foundation of repentance from dead works and of faith toward God.

HEBREWS 6:1

Let the word of Christ dwell in you richly in all wisdom, teaching and admonishing one another in psalms and hymns and spiritual songs, singing with grace in your hearts to the Lord.

COLOSSIANS 3:16

Be diligent to present yourself approved to God, a worker who does not need to be ashamed, rightly dividing the word of truth.

2 TIMOTHY 2:15

The righteous shall flourish like a palm tree,
He shall grow like a cedar in Lebanon.

PSALM 92:12

But we all, with unveiled face, beholding as in a mirror the glory of the Lord, are being transformed into the same image from glory to glory, just as by the Spirit of the Lord.

2 CORINTHIANS 3:18

What You Can Do to Change the World

And He said to them, "Go into all the world and preach the gospel to every creature.

"He who believes and is baptized will be saved; but he who does not believe will be condemned.

"And these signs will follow those who believe: In My name they will cast out demons; they will speak with new tongues; they will take up serpents; and if they drink anything deadly, it will by no means hurt them; they will lay hands on the sick, and they will recover."

So then, after the Lord had spoken to them, He was received up into heaven, and sat down at the right hand of God.

And they went out and preached everywhere, the Lord working with them and confirming the word through the accompanying signs. Amen.

MARK 16:15–20

Most assuredly, I say to you, he who believes in Me, the works that I do he will do also; and greater works than these he will do, because I go to My Father.

JOHN 14:12

You are the light of the world. A city that is set on a hill cannot be hidden.

Nor do they light a lamp and put it under a basket, but on a lampstand, and it gives light to all who are in the house.

Let your light so shine before men, that they may see your good works and glorify your Father in heaven.

MATTHEW 5:14–16

We are of God. He who knows God hears us; he who is not of God does not hear us. By this we know the spirit of truth and the spirit of error.

And we have known and believed the love that God has for us. God is love, and he who abides in love abides in God, and God in him.

Love has been perfected among us in this: that we may have boldness in the day of judgment; because as He is, so are we in this world.

1 JOHN 4:6, 16, 17

Those who are wise shall shine
Like the brightness of the firmament,
And those who turn many to righteousness
Like the stars forever and ever.

DANIEL 12:3

The Spirit of the LORD is upon Me,
Because He has anointed Me
To preach the gospel to the poor;
He has sent Me to heal the brokenhearted,
To proclaim liberty to the captives
And recovery of sight to the blind,
To set at liberty those who are oppressed.

LUKE 4:18

You shall receive power when the Holy Spirit has come upon you; and you shall be witnesses to Me in Jerusalem, and in all Judea and Samaria, and to the end of the earth.

ACTS 1:8

A new commandment I give to you, that you love one another; as I have loved you, that you also love one another.

By this all will know that you are My disciples, if you have love for one another.

JOHN 13:34, 35

What You Can Do to Help Your Business

This Book of the Law shall not depart from your mouth, but you shall meditate in it day and night, that you may observe to do according to all that is written in it. For then you will make your way prosperous, and then you will have good success.

JOSHUA 1:8

Thus says the LORD, your Redeemer,
The Holy One of Israel:
"I am the LORD your God,
Who teaches you to profit,
Who leads you by the way you should go."

ISAIAH 48:17

Beloved, I pray that you may prosper in all things and be in health, just as your soul prospers.

3 JOHN 2

And you shall remember the Lord your God, for it is He who gives you power to get wealth, that He may establish His covenant which He swore to your fathers, as it is this day.

DEUTERONOMY 8:18

Trust in the LORD with all your heart,
And lean not on your own understanding;
In all your ways acknowledge Him,
And He shall direct your paths.
Do not be wise in your own eyes;
Fear the LORD and depart from evil.
It will be health to your flesh,
And strength to your bones.
Honor the LORD with your possessions,
And with the firstfruits of all your increase;
So your barns will be filled with plenty,
And your vats will overflow with new wine.

PROVERBS 3:5–10

Then you will prosper, if you take care to fulfill the statutes and judgments with which the LORD charged Moses concerning Israel. Be strong and of good courage; do not fear nor be dismayed.

1 CHRONICLES 22:13

But seek first the kingdom of God and His right-eousness, and all these things shall be added to you.

MATTHEW 6:33

Commit your works to the LORD,
And your thoughts will be established.

PROVERBS 16:3

Through wisdom a house is built,
And by understanding it is established;
By knowledge the rooms are filled
With all precious and pleasant riches.

PROVERBS 24:3, 4

Not lagging in diligence, fervent in spirit, serving the Lord.

ROMANS 12:11

Masters, give your bondservants what is just and fair, knowing that you also have a Master in heaven.

COLOSSIANS 4:1

What You Can Do to Please God

Everyone who is called by My name,
Whom I have created for My glory;
I have formed him, yes, I have made him.
This people I have formed for Myself;
They shall declare My praise.

ISAIAH 43:7, 21

But the hour is coming, and now is, when the true worshipers will worship the Father in spirit and truth; for the Father is seeking such to worship Him.

God is Spirit, and those who worship Him must worship in spirit and truth.

JOHN 4:23, 24

You also, as living stones, are being built up a spiritual house, a holy priesthood, to offer up spiritual sacrifices acceptable to God through Jesus Christ.

But you are a chosen generation, a royal priesthood, a holy nation, His own special people, that you may proclaim the praises of Him who called you out of darkness into His marvelous light.

1 PETER 2:5, 9

Indeed it came to pass, when the trumpeters and singers were as one, to make one sound to be heard in praising and thanking the LORD, and when they lifted up their voice with the trumpets and cymbals and instruments of music, and praised the LORD, saying: "For He is good, for His mercy endures forever," that the house, the house of the LORD, was filled with a cloud, so that the priests could not continue ministering because of the cloud; for the glory of the LORD filled the house of God.

2 CHRONICLES 5:13, 14

Therefore by Him let us continually offer the sacrifice of praise to God, that is, the fruit of our lips, giving thanks to His name.

But do not forget to do good and to share, for with such sacrifices God is well pleased.

HEBREWS 13:15, 16

You are worthy, O Lord,
To receive glory and honor and power;
For You created all things,
And by Your will they exist and were created.

REVELATION 4:11

That you may walk worthy of the Lord, fully pleasing Him, being fruitful in every good work and increasing in the knowledge of God.

COLOSSIANS 1:10

I beseech you therefore, brethren, by the mercies of God, that you present your bodies a living sacrifice, holy, acceptable to God, which is your reasonable service.

And do not be conformed to this world, but be transformed by the renewing of your mind, that you may prove what is that good and acceptable and perfect will of God.

ROMANS 12:1, 2

Therefore I exhort first of all that supplications, prayers, intercessions, and giving of thanks be made for all men . . .

For this is good and acceptable in the sight of God our Savior.

I desire therefore that the men pray everywhere, lifting up holy hands, without wrath and doubting.

1 TIMOTHY 2:1, 3, 8

GOD'S PLAN OF
SALVATION . . .

GOD'S PLAN OF SALVATION

Moreover, brethren, I declare to you the gospel which I preached to you, which also you received and in which you stand, by which also you are saved, if you hold fast that word which I preached to you—unless you believed in vain.

For I delivered to you first of all that which I also received: that Christ died for our sins according to the Scriptures, and that He was buried, and that He rose again the third day according to the Scriptures.

1 CORINTHIANS 15:1–4

For the wages of sin is death, but the gift of God is eternal life in Christ Jesus our Lord.

ROMANS 6:23

But God demonstrates His own love toward us, in that while we were still sinners, Christ died for us.

ROMANS 5:8

Therefore, just as through one man sin entered the world, and death through sin, and thus death spread to all men, because all sinned.

ROMANS 5:12

And this is the testimony: that God has given us eternal life, and this life is in His Son.

He who has the Son has life; he who does not have the Son of God does not have life.

These things I have written to you who believe in the name of the Son of God, that you may know that you have eternal life, and that you may continue to believe in the name of the Son of God.

1 JOHN 5:11–13

For all have sinned and fall short of the glory of God.

ROMANS 3:23

He who believes in the Son has everlasting life; and he who does not believe the Son shall not see life, but the wrath of God abides on him.

JOHN 3:36

For God did not send His Son into the world to condemn the world, but that the world through Him might be saved.

JOHN 3:17

Therefore whoever confesses Me before men, him I will also confess before My Father who is in heaven.

MATTHEW 10:32

But as many as received Him, to them He gave the right to become children of God, to those who believe in His name.

JOHN 1:12

God so loved the world that He gave His only begotten Son, that whoever believes in Him should not perish but have everlasting life.

JOHN 3:16

For by grace you have been saved through faith, and that not of yourselves; it is the gift of God, not of works, lest anyone should boast.

EPHESIANS 2:8, 9

But what does it say? "The word is near you, in your mouth and in your heart" (that is, the word of faith which we preach): that if you confess with your mouth the Lord Jesus and believe in your heart that God has raised Him from the dead, you will be saved.

For with the heart one believes unto righteousness, and with the mouth confession is made unto salvation.

ROMANS 10:8–10

GOD'S ANSWERS
For Your Life

BEGINNING IN
CHRIST . . .

How to Know You Are Born Again

If you confess with your mouth the Lord Jesus and believe in your heart that God has raised Him from the dead, you will be saved.

For with the heart one believes unto righteousness, and with the mouth confession is made unto salvation.

For the Scripture says, "Whoever believes on Him will not be put to shame."

ROMANS 10:9–11

Most assuredly, I say to you, he who hears My word and believes in Him who sent Me has everlasting life, and shall not come into judgment, but has passed from death into life.

JOHN 5:24

You are all sons of God through faith in Christ Jesus.

For as many of you as were baptized into Christ have put on Christ.

There is neither Jew nor Greek, there is neither slave nor free, there is neither male nor female; for you are all one in Christ Jesus.

GALATIANS 3:26–28

He who received seed on the good ground is he who hears the word and understands it, who indeed bears fruit and produces: some a hundredfold, some sixty, some thirty.

MATTHEW 13:23

Those who are Christ's have crucified the flesh with its passions and desires.

If we live in the Spirit, let us also walk in the Spirit.

GALATIANS 5:24–25

Whoever confesses Me before men, him I will also confess before My Father who is in heaven.

And he who does not take his cross and follow after Me is not worthy of Me.

He who finds his life will lose it, and he who loses his life for My sake will find it.

MATTHEW 10:32, 38–39

I will give you a new heart and put a new spirit within you; I will take the heart of stone out of your flesh and give you a heart of flesh.

I will put My Spirit within you and cause you to walk in My statutes, and you will keep My judgments and do them.

EZEKIEL 36:26–27

I have been crucified with Christ; it is no longer I who live, but Christ lives in me; and the life which I now live in the flesh I live by faith in the Son of God, who loved me and gave Himself for me.

GALATIANS 2:20

Having been born again, not of corruptible seed but incorruptible, through the word of God which lives and abides forever.

1 PETER 1:23

We know that we have passed from death to life, because we love the brethren. He who does not love his brother abides in death.

1 JOHN 3:14

Knowing this, that our old man was crucified with Him, that the body of sin might be done away with, that we should no longer be slaves of sin.

For he who has died has been freed from sin.

Now if we died with Christ, we believe that we shall also live with Him.

ROMANS 6:6–8

HOW TO KNOW THE SUFFICIENCY OF JESUS

Looking unto Jesus, the author and finisher of our faith, who for the joy that was set before Him endured the cross, despising the shame, and has sat down at the right hand of the throne of God.

HEBREWS 12:2

Jesus said to them, "I am the bread of life. He who comes to Me shall never hunger, and he who believes in Me shall never thirst."

JOHN 6:35

Let your conduct be without covetousness; be content with such things as you have. For He Himself has said, "I will never leave you nor forsake you."

So we may boldly say: "The LORD is my helper; I will not fear. What can man do to me?"

Jesus Christ is the same yesterday, today, and forever.

HEBREWS 13:5–6, 8

If the Son makes you free, you shall be free indeed.

JOHN 8:36

I can do all things through Christ who strengthens me.

PHILIPPIANS 4:13

For in Him dwells all the fullness of the Godhead bodily; and you are complete in Him, who is the head of all principality and power.

COLOSSIANS 2:9–10

I am the good shepherd. The good shepherd gives His life for the sheep.

JOHN 10:11

The LORD is my shepherd;
I shall not want.
He makes me to lie down in green pastures;
He leads me beside the still waters.
He restores my soul;
He leads me in the paths of righteousness
For His name's sake.
Yea, though I walk through the valley of the shadow
    of death,
I will fear no evil;
For You are with me;
Your rod and Your staff, they comfort me.

PSALM 23:1–4

We have such trust through Christ toward God.

Not that we are sufficient of ourselves to think of anything as being from ourselves, but our sufficiency is from God.

2 CORINTHIANS 3:4–5

The Lord stood with me and strengthened me, so that the message might be preached fully through me, and that all the Gentiles might hear. Also I was delivered out of the mouth of the lion.

And the Lord will deliver me from every evil work and preserve me for His heavenly kingdom. To Him be glory forever and ever. Amen!

2 TIMOTHY 4:17–18

My help comes from the LORD,
Who made heaven and earth.
He will not allow your foot to be moved;
He who keeps you will not slumber.

PSALM 121:2–3

Jesus said to him, "I am the way, the truth, and the life. No one comes to the Father except through Me."

JOHN 14:6

What the Blood of Jesus Is to You

How much more shall the blood of Christ, who through the eternal Spirit offered Himself without spot to God, cleanse your conscience from dead works to serve the living God?

HEBREWS 9:14

Being justified freely by His grace through the redemption that is in Christ Jesus, whom God set forth as a propitiation by His blood, through faith, to demonstrate His righteousness, because in His forbearance God had passed over the sins that were previously committed, to demonstrate at the present time His righteousness, that He might be just and the justifier of the one who has faith in Jesus.

ROMANS 3:24–26

Then likewise he sprinkled with blood both the tabernacle and all the vessels of the ministry.

And according to the law almost all things are purified with blood, and without shedding of blood there is no remission.

HEBREWS 9:21–22

In Him we have redemption through His blood, the forgiveness of sins, according to the riches of His grace.

EPHESIANS 1:7

This is My blood of the new covenant, which is shed for many for the remission of sins.

MATTHEW 26:28

For the life of the flesh is in the blood, and I have given it to you upon the altar to make atonement for your souls; for it is the blood that makes atonement for the soul.

LEVITICUS 17:11

God demonstrates His own love toward us, in that while we were still sinners, Christ died for us.

Much more then, having now been justified by His blood, we shall be saved from wrath through Him.

For if when we were enemies we were reconciled to God through the death of His Son, much more, having been reconciled, we shall be saved by His life.

ROMANS 5:8–10

If we walk in the light as He is in the light, we have fellowship with one another, and the blood of Jesus Christ His Son cleanses us from all sin.

1 JOHN 1:7

Then Jesus said to them, "Most assuredly, I say to you, unless you eat the flesh of the Son of Man and drink His blood, you have no life in you.

"Whoever eats My flesh and drinks My blood has eternal life, and I will raise him up at the last day.

"He who eats My flesh and drinks My blood abides in Me, and I in him."

JOHN 6:53, 54, 56

Knowing that you were not redeemed with corruptible things, like silver or gold, from your aimless conduct received by tradition from your fathers, but with the precious blood of Christ, as of a lamb without blemish and without spot.

He indeed was foreordained before the foundation of the world, but was manifest in these last times for you who through Him believe in God, who raised Him from the dead and gave Him glory, so that your faith and hope are in God.

1 PETER 1:18–21

How to Know the Power of God's Word

The word of God is living and powerful, and sharper than any two-edged sword, piercing even to the division of soul and spirit, and of joints and marrow, and is a discerner of the thoughts and intents of the heart.

HEBREWS 4:12

As newborn babes, desire the pure milk of the word, that you may grow thereby, if indeed you have tasted that the Lord is gracious.

1 PETER 2:2–3

Your word I have hidden in my heart, that I might not sin against You.

I will delight myself in Your statutes; I will not forget Your word.

PSALM 119:11, 16

Forever, O LORD,
Your word is settled in heaven.
Your faithfulness endures to all generations;
You established the earth, and it abides.

PSALM 119:89–90

By the word of the LORD the heavens were made, and all the host of them by the breath of His mouth.

PSALM 33:6

How sweet are Your words to my taste,
Sweeter than honey to my mouth!
Through Your precepts I get understanding;
Therefore I hate every false way.
Your word is a lamp to my feet
And a light to my path.

PSALM 119:103–105

Your testimonies are wonderful;
Therefore my soul keeps them.
The entrance of Your words gives light;
It gives understanding to the simple.

PSALM 119:129–130

You are already clean because of the word which I have spoken to you.

JOHN 15:3

It is the Spirit who gives life; the flesh profits nothing. The words that I speak to you are spirit, and they are life.

JOHN 6:63

The grass withers, the flower fades,
But the word of our God stands forever.

ISAIAH 40:8

He answered and said, "It is written, 'Man shall not live by bread alone, but by every word that proceeds from the mouth of God.'"

MATTHEW 4:4

Having been born again, not of corruptible seed but incorruptible, through the word of God which lives and abides forever, because "All flesh is as grass, and all the glory of man as the flower of the grass. The grass withers, and its flower falls away, but the word of the LORD endures forever."

Now this is the word which by the gospel was preached to you.

1 PETER 1:23–25

Then Jesus said to those Jews who believed Him, "If you abide in My word, you are My disciples indeed.

"And you shall know the truth, and the truth shall make you free."

JOHN 8:31–32

And being assembled together with them, He commanded them not to depart from Jerusalem, but to wait for the Promise of the Father, "which," He said, "you have heard from Me; "for John truly baptized with water, but you shall be baptized with the Holy Spirit not many days from now."

Therefore, when they had come together, they asked Him, saying, "Lord, will You at this time restore the kingdom to Israel?"

And He said to them, "It is not for you to know times or seasons which the Father has put in His own authority.

"But you shall receive power when the Holy Spirit has come upon you; and you shall be witnesses to Me in Jerusalem, and in all Judea and Samaria, and to the end of the earth."

ACTS 1:4–8

See that you do not refuse Him who speaks. For if they did not escape who refused Him who spoke on earth, much more shall we not escape if we turn away from Him who speaks from heaven.

HEBREWS 12:25

Who also made us sufficient as ministers of the new covenant, not of the letter but of the Spirit; for the letter kills, but the Spirit gives life.

Now the Lord is the Spirit; and where the Spirit of the Lord is, there is liberty.

But we all, with unveiled face, beholding as in a mirror the glory of the Lord, are being transformed into the same image from glory to glory, just as by the Spirit of the Lord.

2 CORINTHIANS 3:6, 17–18

But the fruit of the Spirit is love, joy, peace, longsuffering, kindness, goodness, faithfulness, gentleness, self-control. Against such there is no law.

And those who are Christ's have crucified the flesh with its passions and desires.

If we live in the Spirit, let us also walk in the Spirit.

GALATIANS 5:22–25

It is not you who speak, but the Spirit of your Father who speaks in you.

MATTHEW 10:20

The Holy Spirit will teach you in that very hour what you ought to say.

LUKE 12:12

So shall they fear
The name of the LORD from the west,
And His glory from the rising of the sun;
When the enemy comes in like a flood,
The Spirit of the LORD will lift up a standard against
him.

ISAIAH 59:19

Knowing this first, that no prophecy of Scripture is of
any private interpretation, for prophecy never came
by the will of man, but holy men of God spoke as
they were moved by the Holy Spirit.

2 PETER 1:20–21

But you, beloved, building yourselves up on your
most holy faith, praying in the Holy Spirit, keep
yourselves in the love of God, looking for the mercy
of our Lord Jesus Christ unto eternal life.

JUDE 20, 21

Behold, I send the Promise of My Father upon you;
but tarry in the city of Jerusalem until you are endued
with power from on high.

LUKE 24:49

HOW TO ABIDE IN CHRIST

Abide in Me, and I in you. As the branch cannot bear fruit of itself, unless it abides in the vine, neither can you, unless you abide in Me.

I am the vine, you are the branches. He who abides in Me, and I in him, bears much fruit; for without Me you can do nothing.

If anyone does not abide in Me, he is cast out as a branch and is withered; and they gather them and throw them into the fire, and they are burned.

If you abide in Me, and My words abide in you, you will ask what you desire, and it shall be done for you.

JOHN 15:4–7

And now, little children, abide in Him, that when He appears, we may have confidence and not be ashamed before Him at His coming.

1 JOHN 2:28

I will meditate on Your precepts,
And contemplate Your ways.
I will delight myself in Your statutes;
I will not forget Your word.

PSALM 119:15–16

God's Answers

Draw near to God and He will draw near to you. Cleanse your hands, you sinners; and purify your hearts, you double-minded.

JAMES 4:8

I love those who love me,
And those who seek me diligently will find me.

PROVERBS 8:17

Let the word of Christ dwell in you richly in all wisdom, teaching and admonishing one another in psalms and hymns and spiritual songs, singing with grace in your hearts to the Lord.

COLOSSIANS 3:16

Those who wait on the LORD
Shall renew their strength;
They shall mount up with wings like eagles,
They shall run and not be weary,
They shall walk and not faint.

ISAIAH 40:31

In Him we live and move and have our being, as also some of your own poets have said, "For we are also His offspring."

ACTS 17:28

But put on the Lord Jesus Christ, and make no provision for the flesh, to fulfill its lusts.

ROMANS 13:14

Now by this we know that we know Him, if we keep His commandments.

He who says, "I know Him," and does not keep His commandments, is a liar, and the truth is not in him.

But whoever keeps His word, truly the love of God is perfected in him. By this we know that we are in Him.

He who says he abides in Him ought himself also to walk just as He walked.

1 JOHN 2:3–6

Blessed is the man who listens to me,
Watching daily at my gates,
Waiting at the posts of my doors.

PROVERBS 8:34

As newborn babes, desire the pure milk of the word, that you may grow thereby.

1 PETER 2:2

How to Build Your Faith

Now faith is the substance of things hoped for, the evidence of things not seen.

By faith we understand that the worlds were framed by the word of God, so that the things which are seen were not made of things which are visible.

But without faith it is impossible to please Him, for he who comes to God must believe that He is, and that He is a rewarder of those who diligently seek Him.

By faith he forsook Egypt, not fearing the wrath of the king; for he endured as seeing Him who is invisible.

HEBREWS 11:1, 3, 6, 27

That the genuineness of your faith, being much more precious than gold that perishes, though it is tested by fire, may be found to praise, honor, and glory at the revelation of Jesus Christ, whom having not seen you love. Though now you do not see Him, yet believing, you rejoice with joy inexpressible and full of glory, receiving the end of your faith—the salvation of your souls.

1 PETER 1:7–9

For in it the righteousness of God is revealed from faith to faith; as it is written, "The just shall live by faith."

ROMANS 1:17

So then faith comes by hearing, and hearing by the word of God.

ROMANS 10:17

Have I not commanded you? Be strong and of good courage; do not be afraid, nor be dismayed, for the LORD your God is with you wherever you go.

JOSHUA 1:9

If any of you lacks wisdom, let him ask of God, who gives to all liberally and without reproach, and it will be given to him.

But let him ask in faith, with no doubting, for he who doubts is like a wave of the sea driven and tossed by the wind.

For let not that man suppose that he will receive anything from the Lord; he is a double-minded man, unstable in all his ways.

JAMES 1:5–8

For with God nothing will be impossible.

LUKE 1:37

He did not waver at the promise of God through unbelief, but was strengthened in faith, giving glory to God, and being fully convinced that what He had promised He was also able to perform.

ROMANS 4:20–21

We are hard pressed on every side, yet not crushed; we are perplexed, but not in despair; persecuted, but not forsaken; struck down, but not destroyed—always carrying about in the body the dying of the Lord Jesus, that the life of Jesus also may be manifested in our body.

2 CORINTHIANS 4:8–10

What then shall we say to these things? If God is for us, who can be against us?

ROMANS 8:31

But you, beloved, building yourselves up on your most holy faith, praying in the Holy Spirit, keep yourselves in the love of God, looking for the mercy of our Lord Jesus Christ unto eternal life.

JUDE 20, 21

We walk by faith, not by sight.

2 CORINTHIANS 5:7

GROWING IN
CHRIST . . .

How to Overcome the Carnal Mind

I beseech you therefore, brethren, by the mercies of God, that you present your bodies a living sacrifice, holy, acceptable to God, which is your reasonable service.

And do not be conformed to this world, but be transformed by the renewing of your mind, that you may prove what is that good and acceptable and perfect will of God.

ROMANS 12:1–2

Therefore gird up the loins of your mind, be sober, and rest your hope fully upon the grace that is to be brought to you at the revelation of Jesus Christ; as obedient children, not conforming yourselves to the former lusts, as in your ignorance; but as He who called you is holy, you also be holy in all your conduct.

1 PETER 1:13–15

Therefore we do not lose heart. Even though our outward man is perishing, yet the inward man is being renewed day by day.

2 CORINTHIANS 4:16

For you, brethren, have been called to liberty; only do not use liberty as an opportunity for the flesh, but through love serve one another.

For all the law is fulfilled in one word, even in this: "You shall love your neighbor as yourself."

But if you bite and devour one another, beware lest you be consumed by one another!

I say then: Walk in the Spirit, and you shall not fulfill the lust of the flesh.

For the flesh lusts against the Spirit, and the Spirit against the flesh; and these are contrary to one another, so that you do not do the things that you wish.

GALATIANS 5:13–17

I have been crucified with Christ; it is no longer I who live, but Christ lives in me; and the life which I now live in the flesh I live by faith in the Son of God, who loved me and gave Himself for me.

GALATIANS 2:20

Beware lest anyone cheat you through philosophy and empty deceit, according to the tradition of men, according to the basic principles of the world, and not according to Christ.

COLOSSIANS 2:8

For the law of the Spirit of life in Christ Jesus has made me free from the law of sin and death.

For what the law could not do in that it was weak through the flesh, God did by sending His own Son in the likeness of sinful flesh, on account of sin: He condemned sin in the flesh, that the righteous requirement of the law might be fulfilled in us who do not walk according to the flesh but according to the Spirit.

For those who live according to the flesh set their minds on the things of the flesh, but those who live according to the Spirit, the things of the Spirit.

For to be carnally minded is death, but to be spiritually minded is life and peace.

Because the carnal mind is enmity against God; for it is not subject to the law of God, nor indeed can be.

So then, those who are in the flesh cannot please God.

But you are not in the flesh but in the Spirit, if indeed the Spirit of God dwells in you. Now if anyone does not have the Spirit of Christ, he is not His.

And if Christ is in you, the body is dead because of sin, but the Spirit is life because of righteousness.

But if the Spirit of Him who raised Jesus from the dead dwells in you, He who raised Christ from the dead will also give life to your mortal bodies through His Spirit who dwells in you.

ROMANS 8:2–11

How to Overcome Satan

Be sober, be vigilant; because your adversary the devil walks about like a roaring lion, seeking whom he may devour.

Resist him, steadfast in the faith, knowing that the same sufferings are experienced by your brotherhood in the world.

But may the God of all grace, who called us to His eternal glory by Christ Jesus, after you have suffered a while, perfect, establish, strengthen, and settle you.

1 PETER 5:8–10

He who sins is of the devil, for the devil has sinned from the beginning. For this purpose the Son of God was manifested, that He might destroy the works of the devil.

1 JOHN 3:8

Submit to God. Resist the devil and he will flee from you.

Draw near to God and He will draw near to you. Cleanse your hands, you sinners; and purify your hearts, you double-minded.

JAMES 4:7–8

Surely He shall deliver you from the snare of the
  fowler
And from the perilous pestilence.
He shall cover you with His feathers,
And under His wings you shall take refuge;
His truth shall be your shield and buckler.
You shall not be afraid of the terror by night,
Nor of the arrow that flies by day,
Nor of the pestilence that walks in darkness,
Nor of the destruction that lays waste at noonday.
A thousand may fall at your side,
And ten thousand at your right hand;
But it shall not come near you.

PSALM 91:3–7

The LORD shall preserve you from all evil;
He shall preserve your soul.
The LORD shall preserve your going out and your
  coming in
From this time forth, and even forevermore.

PSALM 121:7–8

In that He Himself has suffered, being tempted, He
is able to aid those who are tempted.

HEBREWS 2:18

And He said to them, "I saw Satan fall like lightning from heaven. Behold, I give you the authority to trample on serpents and scorpions, and over all the power of the enemy, and nothing shall by any means hurt you."

LUKE 10:18–19

Finally, my brethren, be strong in the Lord and in the power of His might.

Put on the whole armor of God, that you may be able to stand against the wiles of the devil.

For we do not wrestle against flesh and blood, but against principalities, against powers, against the rulers of the darkness of this age, against spiritual hosts of wickedness in the heavenly places.

Therefore take up the whole armor of God, that you may be able to withstand in the evil day, and having done all, to stand.

Stand therefore, having girded your waist with truth, having put on the breastplate of righteousness, and having shod your feet with the preparation of the gospel of peace; above all, taking the shield of faith with which you will be able to quench all the fiery darts of the wicked one.

And take the helmet of salvation, and the sword of the Spirit, which is the word of God.

EPHESIANS 6:10–17

Beware of false prophets, who come to you in sheep's clothing, but inwardly they are ravenous wolves.

You will know them by their fruits. Do men gather grapes from thornbushes or figs from thistles?

Even so, every good tree bears good fruit, but a bad tree bears bad fruit.

Therefore by their fruits you will know them.

Not everyone who says to Me, "Lord, Lord," shall enter the kingdom of heaven, but he who does the will of My Father in heaven.

Many will say to Me in that day, "Lord, Lord, have we not prophesied in Your name, cast out demons in Your name, and done many wonders in Your name?"

And then I will declare to them, "I never knew you; depart from Me, you who practice lawlessness!"

MATTHEW 7:15–17, 20–23

"Behold, I am against those who prophesy false dreams," says the LORD, "and tell them, and cause My people to err by their lies and by their recklessness. Yet I did not send them or command them; therefore they shall not profit this people at all," says the LORD.

JEREMIAH 23:32

They profess to know God, but in works they deny Him, being abominable, disobedient, and disqualified for every good work.

TITUS 1:16

Beloved, do not believe every spirit, but test the spirits, whether they are of God; because many false prophets have gone out into the world.

By this you know the Spirit of God: Every spirit that confesses that Jesus Christ has come in the flesh is of God, and every spirit that does not confess that Jesus Christ has come in the flesh is not of God. And this is the spirit of the Antichrist, which you have heard was coming, and is now already in the world.

1 JOHN 4:1–3

And when they say to you, "Seek those who are mediums and wizards, who whisper and mutter," should not a people seek their God? Should they seek the dead on behalf of the living?

To the law and to the testimony! If they do not speak according to this word, it is because there is no light in them.

ISAIAH 8:19–20

Stand fast therefore in the liberty by which Christ has made us free, and do not be entangled again with a yoke of bondage.

GALATIANS 5:1

A good tree does not bear bad fruit, nor does a bad tree bear good fruit.

For every tree is known by its own fruit. For men do not gather figs from thorns, nor do they gather grapes from a bramble bush.

LUKE 6:43–44

For God is not the author of confusion but of peace, as in all the churches of the saints.

1 CORINTHIANS 14:33

God has not given us a spirit of fear, but of power and of love and of a sound mind.

2 TIMOTHY 1:7

He who sins is of the devil, for the devil has sinned from the beginning. For this purpose the Son of God was manifested, that He might destroy the works of the devil.

1 JOHN 3:8

How to Overcome Worldliness

Do not love the world or the things in the world. If anyone loves the world, the love of the Father is not in him.

For all that is in the world—the lust of the flesh, the lust of the eyes, and the pride of life—is not of the Father but is of the world.

And the world is passing away, and the lust of it; but he who does the will of God abides forever.

1 JOHN 2:15–17

Choosing rather to suffer affliction with the people of God than to enjoy the passing pleasures of sin, esteeming the reproach of Christ greater riches than the treasures in Egypt; for he looked to the reward.

By faith he forsook Egypt, not fearing the wrath of the king; for he endured as seeing Him who is invisible.

HEBREWS 11:25–27

The Lord knows how to deliver the godly out of temptations and to reserve the unjust under punishment for the day of judgment.

2 PETER 2:9

Do not be conformed to this world, but be transformed by the renewing of your mind, that you may prove what is that good and acceptable and perfect will of God.

ROMANS 12:2

No one can serve two masters; for either he will hate the one and love the other, or else he will be loyal to the one and despise the other. You cannot serve God and mammon.

MATTHEW 6:24

Then He said to them all, "If anyone desires to come after Me, let him deny himself, and take up his cross daily, and follow Me.

"For whoever desires to save his life will lose it, but whoever loses his life for My sake will save it.

"For what profit is it to a man if he gains the whole world, and is himself destroyed or lost?"

LUKE 9:23–25

By which have been given to us exceedingly great and precious promises, that through these you may be partakers of the divine nature, having escaped the corruption that is in the world through lust.

2 PETER 1:4

And do this, knowing the time, that now it is high time to awake out of sleep; for now our salvation is nearer than when we first believed.

The night is far spent, the day is at hand. Therefore let us cast off the works of darkness, and let us put on the armor of light.

Let us walk properly, as in the day, not in revelry and drunkenness, not in lewdness and lust, not in strife and envy.

But put on the Lord Jesus Christ, and make no provision for the flesh, to fulfill its lusts.

ROMANS 13:11–14

Now therefore, fear the LORD, serve Him in sincerity and in truth, and put away the gods which your fathers served on the other side of the River and in Egypt. Serve the LORD!

JOSHUA 24:14

Take heed to yourselves, lest your hearts be weighed down with carousing, drunkenness, and cares of this life, and that Day come on you unexpectedly.

LUKE 21:34

How to Deal with Lust

Now therefore, listen to me, my children;
Pay attention to the words of my mouth:
Do not let your heart turn aside to her ways,
Do not stray into her paths;
For she has cast down many wounded,
And all who were slain by her were strong men.
Her house is the way to hell,
Descending to the chambers of death.

PROVERBS 7:24–27

I say then: Walk in the Spirit, and you shall not fulfill the lust of the flesh.

For the flesh lusts against the Spirit, and the Spirit against the flesh; and these are contrary to one another, so that you do not do the things that you wish.

GALATIANS 5:16–17

No temptation has overtaken you except such as is common to man; but God is faithful, who will not allow you to be tempted beyond what you are able, but with the temptation will also make the way of escape, that you may be able to bear it.

1 CORINTHIANS 10:13

Put off, concerning your former conduct, the old man which grows corrupt according to the deceitful lusts, and be renewed in the spirit of your mind, and . . . put on the new man which was created according to God, in true righteousness and holiness . . . nor give place to the devil.

EPHESIANS 4:22–24, 27

Do you not know that your bodies are members of Christ? Shall I then take the members of Christ and make them members of a harlot? Certainly not!

Or do you not know that he who is joined to a harlot is one body with her? For "the two," He says, "shall become one flesh."

But he who is joined to the Lord is one spirit with Him.

Flee sexual immorality. Every sin that a man does is outside the body, but he who commits sexual immorality sins against his own body.

Or do you not know that your body is the temple of the Holy Spirit who is in you, whom you have from God, and you are not your own?

For you were bought at a price; therefore glorify God in your body and in your spirit, which are God's.

1 CORINTHIANS 6:15–20

Do not lust after her beauty in your heart,
Nor let her allure you with her eyelids.
For by means of a harlot
A man is reduced to a crust of bread;
And an adulteress will prey upon his precious life.

PROVERBS 6:25–26

My brethren, count it all joy when you fall into various trials, knowing that the testing of your faith produces patience.

But let patience have its perfect work, that you may be perfect and complete, lacking nothing.

JAMES 1:2–4

How to Overcome Pride

Pride goes before destruction,
And a haughty spirit before a fall.
Better to be of a humble spirit with the lowly,
Than to divide the spoil with the proud.
He who heeds the word wisely will find good,
And whoever trusts in the LORD, happy is he.

PROVERBS 16:18–20

He who is of a proud heart stirs up strife,
But he who trusts in the LORD will be prospered.
He who trusts in his own heart is a fool,
But whoever walks wisely will be delivered.

PROVERBS 28:25–26

Then Jesus called a little child to Him, set him in the midst of them, and said, "Assuredly, I say to you, unless you are converted and become as little children, you will by no means enter the kingdom of heaven. Therefore whoever humbles himself as this little child is the greatest in the kingdom of heaven."

MATTHEW 18:2–4

But He gives more grace. Therefore He says: "God resists the proud, but gives grace to the humble."

Therefore submit to God. Resist the devil and he will flee from you.

Humble yourselves in the sight of the Lord, and He will lift you up.

JAMES 4:6–7, 10

Yet it shall not be so among you; but whoever desires to become great among you, let him be your servant

And whoever desires to be first among you, let him be your slave.

MATTHEW 20:26–27

Likewise you younger people, submit yourselves to your elders. Yes, all of you be submissive to one another, and be clothed with humility, for "God resists the proud, but gives grace to the humble."

Therefore humble yourselves under the mighty hand of God, that He may exalt you in due time.

1 PETER 5:5–6

But we have this treasure in earthen vessels, that the excellence of the power may be of God and not of us.

2 CORINTHIANS 4:7

How to Overcome Pride

Hear and give ear:
Do not be proud,
For the LORD has spoken.
Give glory to the LORD your God
Before He causes darkness,
And before your feet stumble
On the dark mountains,
And while you are looking for light,
He turns it into the shadow of death
And makes it dense darkness.
But if you will not hear it,
My soul will weep in secret for your pride;
My eyes will weep bitterly
And run down with tears,
Because the LORD's flock has been taken captive.

JEREMIAH 13:15–17

Take My yoke upon you and learn from Me, for I am gentle and lowly in heart, and you will find rest for your souls.

For My yoke is easy and My burden is light.

MATTHEW 11:29–30

The fear of the LORD is the instruction of wisdom,
And before honor is humility.

PROVERBS 15:33

How to Control Your Tongue

Death and life are in the power of the tongue,
And those who love it will eat its fruit.

PROVERBS 18:21

Let no corrupt word proceed out of your mouth, but what is good for necessary edification, that it may impart grace to the hearers.

Let all bitterness, wrath, anger, clamor, and evil speaking be put away from you, with all malice.

And be kind to one another, tenderhearted, forgiving one another, even as God in Christ forgave you.

EPHESIANS 4:29, 31–32

Pleasant words are like a honeycomb,
Sweetness to the soul and health to the bones.

PROVERBS 16:24

O Timothy! Guard what was committed to your trust, avoiding the profane and idle babblings and contradictions of what is falsely called knowledge—by professing it some have strayed concerning the faith. Grace be with you. Amen.

1 TIMOTHY 6:20–21

He who guards his mouth preserves his life, but he who opens wide his lips shall have destruction.

PROVERBS 13:3

A good man out of the good treasure of his heart brings forth good; and an evil man out of the evil treasure of his heart brings forth evil. For out of the abundance of the heart his mouth speaks.

LUKE 6:45

But I say to you that for every idle word men may speak, they will give account of it in the day of judgment.

MATTHEW 12:36

Sing to Him, sing psalms to Him; talk of all His wondrous works!

1 CHRONICLES 16:9

Whoever guards his mouth and tongue keeps his soul from troubles.

PROVERBS 21:23

Do not be a witness against your neighbor without cause, for would you deceive with your lips?

PROVERBS 24:28

Avoid foolish disputes, genealogies, contentions, and strivings about the law; for they are unprofitable and useless.

TITUS 3:9

> As long as my breath is in me,
> And the breath of God in my nostrils,
> My lips will not speak wickedness,
> Nor my tongue utter deceit.

JOB 27:3–4

As He who called you is holy, you also be holy in all your conduct.

1 PETER 1:15

Who, when He was reviled, did not revile in return; when He suffered, He did not threaten, but committed Himself to Him who judges righteously.

1 PETER 2:23

He who would love life and see good days, let him refrain his tongue from evil, and his lips from speaking deceit.

1 PETER 3:10

How to Be Christ-Centered

Let the word of Christ dwell in you richly in all wisdom, teaching and admonishing one another in psalms and hymns and spiritual songs, singing with grace in your hearts to the Lord.

And whatever you do in word or deed, do all in the name of the Lord Jesus, giving thanks to God the Father through Him.

COLOSSIANS 3:16–17

I love those who love me,
And those who seek me diligently will find me.

PROVERBS 8:17

Seek the LORD and His strength;
Seek His face evermore!
Remember His marvelous works which He has done,
His wonders, and the judgments of His mouth.

1 CHRONICLES 16:11–12

Trust in Him at all times, you people; pour out your heart before Him; God is a refuge for us.

PSALM 62:8

You are My friends if you do whatever I command you.

No longer do I call you servants, for a servant does not know what his master is doing; but I have called you friends, for all things that I heard from My Father I have made known to you.

You did not choose Me, but I chose you and appointed you that you should go and bear fruit, and that your fruit should remain, that whatever you ask the Father in My name He may give you.

JOHN 15:14–16

Speaking to one another in psalms and hymns and spiritual songs, singing and making melody in your heart to the Lord, giving thanks always for all things to God the Father in the name of our Lord Jesus Christ.

EPHESIANS 5:19–20

I will bless the LORD at all times;
His praise shall continually be in my mouth.
My soul shall make its boast in the LORD;
The humble shall hear of it and be glad.
Oh, magnify the LORD with me,
And let us exalt His name together.
I sought the LORD, and He heard me,
And delivered me from all my fears.

PSALM 34:1–4

Truly my soul silently waits for God;
From Him comes my salvation.
He only is my rock and my salvation;
He is my defense;
I shall not be greatly moved.
My soul, wait silently for God alone,
For my expectation is from Him.
He only is my rock and my salvation;
He is my defense;
I shall not be moved.
In God is my salvation and my glory;
The rock of my strength,
And my refuge, is in God.

PSALM 62:1–2, 5–7

Put on the Lord Jesus Christ, and make no provision
for the flesh, to fulfill its lusts.

ROMANS 13:14

In You, O LORD, I put my trust;
Let me never be put to shame.
For You are my hope, O Lord GOD;
You are my trust from my youth.
Let my mouth be filled with Your praise
And with Your glory all the day.

PSALM 71:1, 5, 8

UNDERSTANDING THE LIBERTY THAT IS IN CHRIST

There is therefore now no condemnation to those who are in Christ Jesus, who do not walk according to the flesh, but according to the Spirit.

For the law of the Spirit of life in Christ Jesus has made me free from the law of sin and death.

ROMANS 8:1–2

For you, brethren, have been called to liberty; only do not use liberty as an opportunity for the flesh, but through love serve one another.

GALATIANS 5:13

There is neither Jew nor Greek, there is neither slave nor free, there is neither male nor female; for you are all one in Christ Jesus.

GALATIANS 3:28

But he who looks into the perfect law of liberty and continues in it, and is not a forgetful hearer but a doer of the work, this one will be blessed in what he does.

JAMES 1:25

Now the Lord is the Spirit; and where the Spirit of the Lord is, there is liberty.

2 CORINTHIANS 3:17

"I, Jesus, have sent My angel to testify to you these things in the churches. I am the Root and the Off-spring of David, the Bright and Morning Star."

And the Spirit and the bride say, "Come!" And let him who hears say, "Come!" And let him who thirsts come. Whoever desires, let him take the water of life freely.

REVELATION 22:16–17

"And you shall know the truth, and the truth shall make you free."

They answered Him, "We are Abraham's descendants, and have never been in bondage to anyone. How can you say, 'You will be made free'?"

Jesus answered them, "Most assuredly, I say to you, whoever commits sin is a slave of sin.

"And a slave does not abide in the house forever, but a son abides forever.

"Therefore if the Son makes you free, you shall be free indeed."

JOHN 8:32–36

Stand fast therefore in the liberty by which Christ has made us free, and do not be entangled again with a yoke of bondage.

GALATIANS 5:1

Am I not an apostle? Am I not free? Have I not seen Jesus Christ our Lord? Are you not my work in the Lord?

1 CORINTHIANS 9:1

Now the Lord is the Spirit; and where the Spirit of the Lord is, there is liberty.

2 CORINTHIANS 3:17

Because the creation itself also will be delivered from the bondage of corruption into the glorious liberty of the children of God.

ROMANS 8:21

How to Praise the Lord

Because Your lovingkindness is better than life,
My lips shall praise You.
Thus I will bless You while I live;
I will lift up my hands in Your name.
My soul shall be satisfied as with marrow and fatness,
And my mouth shall praise You with joyful lips.

PSALM 63:3–5

Praise the LORD!
Sing to the LORD a new song,
And His praise in the assembly of saints.
Let Israel rejoice in their Maker;
Let the children of Zion be joyful in their King.
Let them praise His name with the dance;
Let them sing praises to Him with the timbrel and
  harp.
For the LORD takes pleasure in His people;
He will beautify the humble with salvation.
Let the saints be joyful in glory;
Let them sing aloud on their beds.
Let the high praises of God be in their mouth,
And a two-edged sword in their hand.

PSALM 149:1–6

Whoever offers praise glorifies Me; and to him who orders his conduct aright I will show the salvation of God.

PSALM 50:23

Praise the LORD!
Praise God in His sanctuary;
Praise Him in His mighty firmament!
Praise Him for His mighty acts;
Praise Him according to His excellent greatness!
Praise Him with the sound of the trumpet;
Praise Him with the lute and harp!
Praise Him with the timbrel and dance;
Praise Him with stringed instruments and flutes!
Praise Him with loud cymbals;
Praise Him with clashing cymbals!
Let everything that has breath praise the LORD.
Praise the LORD!

PSALM 150:1–6

You are a chosen generation, a royal priesthood, a holy nation, His own special people, that you may proclaim the praises of Him who called you out of darkness into His marvelous light.

1 PETER 2:9

Accept, I pray, the freewill offerings of my mouth, O
LORD, and teach me Your judgments.

PSALM 119:108

At midnight Paul and Silas were praying and singing
hymns to God, and the prisoners were listening to
them.

ACTS 16:25

Praise the LORD!
Praise, O servants of the LORD,
Praise the name of the LORD!
Blessed be the name of the LORD
From this time forth and forevermore!
From the rising of the sun to its going down
The LORD's name is to be praised.

PSALM 113:1–3

"The voice of joy and the voice of gladness, the voice of
the bridegroom and the voice of the bride, the voice of
those who will say: 'Praise the LORD of hosts, for the
LORD is good, for His mercy endures forever'—and of
those who will bring the sacrifice of praise into the
house of the LORD. For I will cause the captives of the
land to return as at the first," says the LORD.

JEREMIAH 33:11

How to Have the Joy of the Lord

His lord said to him, "Well done, good and faithful servant; you were faithful over a few things, I will make you ruler over many things. Enter into the joy of your lord."

MATTHEW 25:21

And you became followers of us and of the Lord, having received the word in much affliction, with joy of the Holy Spirit.

1 THESSALONIANS 1:6

Let all those rejoice who put their trust in You;
Let them ever shout for joy, because You defend them;
Let those also who love Your name
Be joyful in You.
For You, O LORD, will bless the righteous;
With favor You will surround him as with a shield.

PSALM 5:11–12

A merry heart makes a cheerful countenance, but by sorrow of the heart the spirit is broken.

PROVERBS 15:13

These things I have spoken to you, that My joy may remain in you, and that your joy may be full.

This is My commandment, that you love one another as I have loved you.

JOHN 15:11–12

God has not given us a spirit of fear, but of power and of love and of a sound mind.

2 TIMOTHY 1:7

The kingdom of God is not eating and drinking, but righteousness and peace and joy in the Holy Spirit.

For he who serves Christ in these things is acceptable to God and approved by men.

ROMANS 14:17–18

"Nevertheless do not rejoice in this, that the spirits are subject to you, but rather rejoice because your names are written in heaven."

In that hour Jesus rejoiced in the Spirit and said, "I thank You, Father, Lord of heaven and earth, that You have hidden these things from the wise and prudent and revealed them to babes. Even so, Father, for so it seemed good in Your sight."

LUKE 10:20–21

A merry heart does good, like medicine,
But a broken spirit dries the bones.

PROVERBS 17:22

You love righteousness and hate wickedness;
Therefore God, Your God, has anointed You
With the oil of gladness more than Your companions.
All Your garments are scented with myrrh and aloes
    and cassia,
Out of the ivory palaces, by which they have made
    You glad.

PSALM 45:7–8

Restore to me the joy of Your salvation,
And uphold me by Your generous Spirit.
Then I will teach transgressors Your ways,
And sinners shall be converted to You.

PSALM 51:12–13

This is the day the LORD has made;
We will rejoice and be glad in it.

PSALM 118:24

MATURING IN
CHRIST . . .

How to Handle Spiritual Trials

Beloved, do not think it strange concerning the fiery trial which is to try you, as though some strange thing happened to you; but rejoice to the extent that you partake of Christ's sufferings, that when His glory is revealed, you may also be glad with exceeding joy.

Yet if anyone suffers as a Christian, let him not be ashamed, but let him glorify God in this matter.

1 PETER 4:12–13, 16

But He knows the way that I take;
When He has tested me, I shall come forth as gold.
My foot has held fast to His steps;
I have kept His way and not turned aside.

JOB 23:10–11

The righteous cry out, and the LORD hears,
And delivers them out of all their troubles.
The LORD is near to those who have a broken heart,
And saves such as have a contrite spirit.
Many are the afflictions of the righteous,
But the LORD delivers him out of them all.

PSALM 34:17–19

For You will light my lamp;
The LORD my God will enlighten my darkness.
For by You I can run against a troop,
By my God I can leap over a wall.
As for God, His way is perfect;
The word of the LORD is proven;
He is a shield to all who trust in Him.
It is God who arms me with strength,
And makes my way perfect.

PSALM 18:28–30, 32

Blessed is the man who endures temptation; for when
he has been approved, he will receive the crown of life
which the Lord has promised to those who love Him.

JAMES 1:12

When you pass through the waters, I will be with you;
And through the rivers, they shall not overflow you.
When you walk through the fire, you shall not be
    burned,
Nor shall the flame scorch you.
For I am the LORD your God,
The Holy One of Israel, your Savior;
I gave Egypt for your ransom,
Ethiopia and Seba in your place.

ISAIAH 43:2–3

Though He slay me, yet will I trust Him.
Even so, I will defend my own ways before Him.
He also shall be my salvation,
For a hypocrite could not come before Him.

JOB 13:15–16

Deliver me out of the mire,
And let me not sink;
Let me be delivered from those who hate me,
And out of the deep waters.
Let not the floodwater overflow me,
Nor let the deep swallow me up;
And let not the pit shut its mouth on me.
Hear me, O LORD, for Your lovingkindness is good;
Turn to me according to the multitude of Your tender
   mercies.
And do not hide Your face from Your servant,
For I am in trouble;
Hear me speedily.
Draw near to my soul, and redeem it;
Deliver me because of my enemies.

PSALM 69:14–18

How to Face Serious Illness

Is anyone among you sick? Let him call for the elders of the church, and let them pray over him, anointing him with oil in the name of the Lord.

And the prayer of faith will save the sick, and the Lord will raise him up. And if he has committed sins, he will be forgiven.

JAMES 5:14–15

You will keep him in perfect peace,
Whose mind is stayed on You,
Because he trusts in You.
Trust in the LORD forever,
For in YAH, the LORD, is everlasting strength.

ISAIAH 26:3–4

Heal me, O LORD, and I shall be healed; save me, and I shall be saved, for You are my praise.

JEREMIAH 17:14

Who Himself bore our sins in His own body on the tree, that we, having died to sins, might live for righteousness—by whose stripes you were healed.

1 PETER 2:24

For all things are for your sakes, that grace, having spread through the many, may cause thanksgiving to abound to the glory of God.

Therefore we do not lose heart. Even though our outward man is perishing, yet the inward man is being renewed day by day.

For our light affliction, which is but for a moment, is working for us a far more exceeding and eternal weight of glory, while we do not look at the things which are seen, but at the things which are not seen. For the things which are seen are temporary, but the things which are not seen are eternal.

2 CORINTHIANS 4:15–18

And I said, "This is my anguish;
But I will remember the years of the right hand of the
   Most High."
I will remember the works of the LORD;
Surely I will remember Your wonders of old.
I will also meditate on all Your work,
And talk of Your deeds.
Your way, O God, is in the sanctuary;
Who is so great a God as our God?
You are the God who does wonders;
You have declared Your strength among the peoples.

PSALM 77:10–14

Yea, though I walk through the valley of the shadow of death, I will fear no evil; for You are with me; Your rod and Your staff, they comfort me.

PSALM 23:4

For we know that if our earthly house, this tent, is destroyed, we have a building from God, a house not made with hands, eternal in the heavens.

2 CORINTHIANS 5:1

For this is God, our God forever and ever;
He will be our guide even to death.

PSALM 48:14

But God will redeem my soul from the power of the grave, for He shall receive me.

PSALM 49:15

I call to remembrance my song in the night; I meditate within my heart, and my spirit makes diligent search.

PSALM 77:6

How to Handle Suffering

Therefore, since Christ suffered for us in the flesh, arm yourselves also with the same mind, for he who has suffered in the flesh has ceased from sin, that he no longer should live the rest of his time in the flesh for the lusts of men, but for the will of God.

Beloved, do not think it strange concerning the fiery trial which is to try you, as though some strange thing happened to you; but rejoice to the extent that you partake of Christ's sufferings, that when His glory is revealed, you may also be glad with exceeding joy.

If you are reproached for the name of Christ, blessed are you, for the Spirit of glory and of God rests upon you. On their part He is blasphemed, but on your part He is glorified.

But let none of you suffer as a murderer, a thief, an evildoer, or as a busybody in other people's matters.

Yet if anyone suffers as a Christian, let him not be ashamed, but let him glorify God in this matter.

For the time has come for judgment to begin at the house of God; and if it begins with us first, what will be the end of those who do not obey the gospel of God?

1 Peter 4:1–2, 12–17

You therefore must endure hardship as a good soldier of Jesus Christ.

2 TIMOTHY 2:3

For whom the LORD loves He chastens, and scourges every son whom He receives.

If you endure chastening, God deals with you as with sons; for what son is there whom a father does not chasten?

But if you are without chastening, of which all have become partakers, then you are illegitimate and not sons.

Now no chastening seems to be joyful for the present, but painful; nevertheless, afterward it yields the peaceable fruit of righteousness to those who have been trained by it.

Therefore strengthen the hands which hang down, and the feeble knees, and make straight paths for your feet, so that what is lame may not be dislocated, but rather be healed.

HEBREWS 12:6–8, 11–13

Blessed is the man who endures temptation; for when he has been approved, he will receive the crown of life which the Lord has promised to those who love Him.

JAMES 1:12

For what credit is it if, when you are beaten for your faults, you take it patiently? But when you do good and suffer, if you take it patiently, this is commendable before God.

For to this you were called, because Christ also suffered for us, leaving us an example, that you should follow His steps.

1 PETER 2:20–21

We see Jesus, who was made a little lower than the angels, for the suffering of death crowned with glory and honor, that He, by the grace of God, might taste death for everyone.

For it was fitting for Him, for whom are all things and by whom are all things, in bringing many sons to glory, to make the captain of their salvation perfect through sufferings.

HEBREWS 2:9–10

If children, then heirs—heirs of God and joint heirs with Christ, if indeed we suffer with Him, that we may also be glorified together.

For I consider that the sufferings of this present time are not worthy to be compared with the glory which shall be revealed in us.

ROMANS 8:17–18

How to Survive
Financial Problems

The love of money is a root of all kinds of evil, for which some have strayed from the faith in their greediness, and pierced themselves through with many sorrows.

But you, O man of God, flee these things and pursue righteousness, godliness, faith, love, patience, gentleness.

1 Timothy 6:10–11

Not that I speak in regard to need, for I have learned in whatever state I am, to be content: I know how to be abased, and I know how to abound. Everywhere and in all things I have learned both to be full and to be hungry, both to abound and to suffer need.

I can do all things through Christ who strengthens me.

Philippians 4:11–13

Remove falsehood and lies far from me; give me neither poverty nor riches—feed me with the food allotted to me.

Proverbs 30:8

Trust in the LORD, and do good;
Dwell in the land, and feed on His faithfulness.
Delight yourself also in the LORD,
And He shall give you the desires of your heart.

PSALM 37:3–4

Command those who are rich in this present age not to be haughty, nor to trust in uncertain riches but in the living God, who gives us richly all things to enjoy.

Let them do good, that they be rich in good works, ready to give, willing to share, storing up for themselves a good foundation for the time to come, that they may lay hold on eternal life.

1 TIMOTHY 6:17–19

Then He said to His disciples, "Therefore I say to you, do not worry about your life, what you will eat; nor about the body, what you will put on.

"Life is more than food, and the body is more than clothing.

"Consider the ravens, for they neither sow nor reap, which have neither storehouse nor barn; and God feeds them. Of how much more value are you than the birds?"

LUKE 12:22–24

So we may boldly say: "The LORD is my helper; I will not fear. What can man do to me?"

HEBREWS 13:6

My God shall supply all your need according to His riches in glory by Christ Jesus.

PHILIPPIANS 4:19

He who trusts in his riches will fall,
But the righteous will flourish like foliage.

PROVERBS 11:28

There is one who makes himself rich, yet has nothing; and one who makes himself poor, yet has great riches.
Wealth gained by dishonesty will be diminished, but he who gathers by labor will increase.

PROVERBS 13:7, 11

For you have need of endurance, so that after you have done the will of God, you may receive the promise.

HEBREWS 10:36

Listen, my beloved brethren: Has God not chosen the poor of this world to be rich in faith and heirs of the kingdom which He promised to those who love Him?

JAMES 2:5

How to Handle Stress

Be anxious for nothing, but in everything by prayer and supplication, with thanksgiving, let your requests be made known to God; and the peace of God, which surpasses all understanding, will guard your hearts and minds through Christ Jesus.

Finally, brethren, whatever things are true, whatever things are noble, whatever things are just, whatever things are pure, whatever things are lovely, whatever things are of good report, if there is any virtue and if there is anything praiseworthy—meditate on these things.

PHILIPPIANS 4:6–8

Fear not, for I am with you;
Be not dismayed, for I am your God.
I will strengthen you,
Yes, I will help you,
I will uphold you with My righteous right hand.

ISAIAH 41:10

"Be angry, and do not sin": do not let the sun go down on your wrath, nor give place to the devil.

EPHESIANS 4:26–27

Surely He shall deliver you from the snare of the
  fowler
And from the perilous pestilence.
He shall cover you with His feathers,
And under His wings you shall take refuge;
His truth shall be your shield and buckler.
You shall not be afraid of the terror by night,
Nor of the arrow that flies by day,
Nor of the pestilence that walks in darkness,
Nor of the destruction that lays waste at noonday.
A thousand may fall at your side,
And ten thousand at your right hand;
But it shall not come near you.

PSALM 91:3–7

He makes me to lie down in green pastures;
He leads me beside the still waters.
He restores my soul;
He leads me in the paths of righteousness
For His name's sake.
Yea, though I walk through the valley of the shadow
  of death,
I will fear no evil;
For You are with me;
Your rod and Your staff, they comfort me.

PSALM 23:2–4

Casting all your care upon Him, for He cares for you.

Be sober, be vigilant; because your adversary the devil walks about like a roaring lion, seeking whom he may devour.

Resist him, steadfast in the faith, knowing that the same sufferings are experienced by your brotherhood in the world.

But may the God of all grace, who called us to His eternal glory by Christ Jesus, after you have suffered a while, perfect, establish, strengthen, and settle you.

1 PETER 5:7–10

God is our refuge and strength,
A very present help in trouble.
Therefore we will not fear,
Even though the earth be removed,
And though the mountains be carried into the midst of the sea;
Though its waters roar and be troubled,
Though the mountains shake with its swelling. Selah

PSALM 46:1–3

Peace I leave with you, My peace I give to you; not as the world gives do I give to you. Let not your heart be troubled, neither let it be afraid.

JOHN 14:27

But He was in the stern, asleep on a pillow. And they awoke Him and said to Him, "Teacher, do You not care that we are perishing?"

Then He arose and rebuked the wind, and said to the sea, "Peace, be still!" And the wind ceased and there was a great calm.

But He said to them, "Why are you so fearful? How is it that you have no faith?"

MARK 4:38–40

Whenever I am afraid,
I will trust in You.
In God (I will praise His word),
In God I have put my trust;
I will not fear.
What can flesh do to me?

PSALM 56:3–4

How to Overcome Despair

For His anger is but for a moment,
His favor is for life;
Weeping may endure for a night,
But joy comes in the morning.
I cried out to You, O LORD;
And to the LORD I made supplication:
"What profit is there in my blood,
When I go down to the pit?
Will the dust praise You?
Will it declare Your truth?
Hear, O LORD, and have mercy on me;
LORD, be my helper!"
You have turned for me my mourning into dancing;
You have put off my sackcloth and clothed me with
    gladness,
To the end that my glory may sing praise to You and
    not be silent.
O LORD my God, I will give thanks to You forever.

PSALM 30:5, 8–12

Come to Me, all you who labor and are heavy laden,
and I will give you rest.

MATTHEW 11:28

We are hard pressed on every side, yet not crushed; we are perplexed, but not in despair; persecuted, but not forsaken; struck down, but not destroyed—

Therefore we do not lose heart. Even though our outward man is perishing, yet the inward man is being renewed day by day.

For our light affliction, which is but for a moment, is working for us a far more exceeding and eternal weight of glory, while we do not look at the things which are seen, but at the things which are not seen. For the things which are seen are temporary, but the things which are not seen are eternal.

2 CORINTHIANS 4:8–9, 16–18

Let your conduct be without covetousness; be content with such things as you have. For He Himself has said, "I will never leave you nor forsake you." So we may boldly say: "The LORD is my helper; I will not fear. What can man do to me?"

HEBREWS 13:5–6

This hope we have as an anchor of the soul, both sure and steadfast, and which enters the Presence behind the veil.

HEBREWS 6:19

Finally, brethren, whatever things are true, whatever things are noble, whatever things are just, whatever things are pure, whatever things are lovely, whatever things are of good report, if there is any virtue and if there is anything praiseworthy—meditate on these things.

PHILIPPIANS 4:8

He has not dealt with us according to our sins,
Nor punished us according to our iniquities.
For as the heavens are high above the earth,
So great is His mercy toward those who fear Him;
As far as the east is from the west,
So far has He removed our transgressions from us.

PSALM 103:10–12

After he had patiently endured, he obtained the promise.

HEBREWS 6:15

Let us not grow weary while doing good, for in due season we shall reap if we do not lose heart.

GALATIANS 6:9

How to Maintain Hope

Through the LORD's mercies we are not consumed,
Because His compassions fail not.
They are new every morning;
Great is Your faithfulness.
"The LORD is my portion," says my soul,
"Therefore I hope in Him!"

LAMENTATIONS 3:22–24

But let us who are of the day be sober, putting on the breastplate of faith and love, and as a helmet the hope of salvation.

For God did not appoint us to wrath, but to obtain salvation through our Lord Jesus Christ.

1 THESSALONIANS 5:8–9

Therefore do not worry about tomorrow, for tomorrow will worry about its own things. Sufficient for the day is its own trouble.

MATTHEW 6:34

You are my hiding place and my shield;
I hope in Your word.

PSALM 119:114

Behold, the eye of the LORD is on those who fear
  Him,
On those who hope in His mercy,
To deliver their soul from death,
And to keep them alive in famine.
Our soul waits for the LORD;
He is our help and our shield.
For our heart shall rejoice in Him,
Because we have trusted in His holy name.
Let Your mercy, O LORD, be upon us,
Just as we hope in You.

PSALM 33:18–22

Let your conduct be without covetousness; be content with such things as you have. For He Himself has said, "I will never leave you nor forsake you."

So we may boldly say: "The LORD is my helper; I will not fear. What can man do to me?"

HEBREWS 13:5–6

Now may the God of hope fill you with all joy and peace in believing, that you may abound in hope by the power of the Holy Spirit.

ROMANS 15:13

How to Maintain Hope

Cast your burden on the LORD,
And He shall sustain you;
He shall never permit the righteous to be moved.

PSALM 55:22

My soul, wait silently for God alone,
For my expectation is from Him.
He only is my rock and my salvation;
He is my defense;
I shall not be moved.
In God is my salvation and my glory;
The rock of my strength,
And my refuge, is in God.

PSALM 62:5–7

Those who wait on the LORD
Shall renew their strength;
They shall mount up with wings like eagles,
They shall run and not be weary,
They shall walk and not faint.

ISAIAH 40:31

HOW TO ENTER INTO GOD'S REST

Commit your way to the LORD,
Trust also in Him,
And He shall bring it to pass.
He shall bring forth your righteousness as the light,
And your justice as the noonday.
Rest in the LORD, and wait patiently for Him;
Do not fret because of him who prospers in his way,
Because of the man who brings wicked schemes to
    pass.

PSALM 37:5–7

There remains therefore a rest for the people of God.

Let us therefore be diligent to enter that rest, lest
anyone fall according to the same example of
disobedience.

Seeing then that we have a great High Priest who
has passed through the heavens, Jesus the Son of God,
let us hold fast our confession.

HEBREWS 4:9, 11, 14

He said, "My Presence will go with you, and I will
give you rest."

EXODUS 33:14

Therefore, having been justified by faith, we have peace with God through our Lord Jesus Christ, through whom also we have access by faith into this grace in which we stand, and rejoice in hope of the glory of God.

ROMANS 5:1–2

We know that all things work together for good to those who love God, to those who are the called according to His purpose.

ROMANS 8:28

God is not the author of confusion but of peace, as in all the churches of the saints.

1 CORINTHIANS 14:33

Cast your burden on the LORD, and He shall sustain you; He shall never permit the righteous to be moved.

PSALM 55:22

The fear of man brings a snare,
But whoever trusts in the LORD shall be safe.

PROVERBS 29:25

HOW TO BE ESTABLISHED IN TRUST

Blessed is the man who trusts in the LORD,
And whose hope is the LORD.
For he shall be like a tree planted by the waters,
Which spreads out its roots by the river,
And will not fear when heat comes;
But its leaf will be green,
And will not be anxious in the year of drought,
Nor will cease from yielding fruit.

JEREMIAH 17:7–8

We know that all things work together for good to those who love God, to those who are the called according to His purpose.

ROMANS 8:28

Casting all your care upon Him, for He cares for you.
1 PETER 5:7

Therefore we will not fear, even though the earth be removed, and though the mountains be carried into the midst of the sea.

PSALM 46:2

I will say of the LORD, "He is my refuge and my
    fortress;
My God, in Him I will trust."
Surely He shall deliver you from the snare of the
    fowler
And from the perilous pestilence.
He shall cover you with His feathers,
He will not be afraid of evil tidings;
His heart is steadfast, trusting in the LORD.
His heart is established;
He will not be afraid,
Until he sees his desire upon his enemies.
And under His wings you shall take refuge;
His truth shall be your shield and buckler.

PSALM 91:2–4

PSALM 112:7–8

Yes, we had the sentence of death in ourselves, that
we should not trust in ourselves but in God who
raises the dead, who delivered us from so great a
death, and does deliver us; in whom we trust that He
will still deliver us.

2 CORINTHIANS 1:9–10

Through God we will do valiantly,
For it is He who shall tread down our enemies.

PSALM 60:12

The LORD is on my side;
I will not fear.
What can man do to me?
It is better to trust in the LORD
Than to put confidence in man.

PSALM 118:6, 8

He will not allow your foot to be moved;
He who keeps you will not slumber.

PSALM 121:3

Those who trust in the LORD
Are like Mount Zion,
Which cannot be moved, but abides forever.
Do good, O LORD, to those who are good,
And to those who are upright in their hearts.

PSALM 125:1, 4

He who heeds the word wisely will find good,
And whoever trusts in the LORD, happy is he.

PROVERBS 16:20

How to Face Old Age

The righteous shall flourish like a palm tree,
He shall grow like a cedar in Lebanon.
Those who are planted in the house of the LORD
Shall flourish in the courts of our God.
They shall still bear fruit in old age;
They shall be fresh and flourishing,
To declare that the LORD is upright;
He is my rock, and there is no unrighteousness in Him.

PSALM 92:12–15

For by me your days will be multiplied,
And years of life will be added to you.

PROVERBS 9:11

Who satisfies your mouth with good things,
So that your youth is renewed like the eagle's.

PSALM 103:5

None of us lives to himself, and no one dies to himself.
For if we live, we live to the Lord; and if we die, we
die to the Lord. Therefore, whether we live or die, we
are the Lord's.

ROMANS 14:7–8

The days of our lives are seventy years;
And if by reason of strength they are eighty years,
Yet their boast is only labor and sorrow;
For it is soon cut off, and we fly away.
So teach us to number our days,
That we may gain a heart of wisdom.
Oh, satisfy us early with Your mercy,
That we may rejoice and be glad all our days!

PSALM 90:10, 12, 14

For I know that my Redeemer lives,
And He shall stand at last on the earth;
And after my skin is destroyed, this I know,
That in my flesh I shall see God,
Whom I shall see for myself,
And my eyes shall behold, and not another.
How my heart yearns within me!

JOB 19:25–27

That the older men be sober, reverent, temperate, sound in faith, in love, in patience; the older women likewise, that they be reverent in behavior, not slanderers, not given to much wine, teachers of good things—that they admonish the young women to love their husbands, to love their children.

TITUS 2:2–4

For this is God, our God forever and ever;
He will be our guide even to death.

PSALM 48:14

The fear of the LORD prolongs days,
But the years of the wicked will be shortened.

PROVERBS 10:27

You shall come to the grave at a full age, as a sheaf of grain ripens in its season.

JOB 5:26

For we know that if our earthly house, this tent, is destroyed, we have a building from God, a house not made with hands, eternal in the heavens.

2 CORINTHIANS 5:1

We do not look at the things which are seen, but at the things which are not seen. For the things which are seen are temporary, but the things which are not seen are eternal.

2 CORINTHIANS 4:18

How to Have God's Divine Protection

When you pass through the waters, I will be with you;
And through the rivers, they shall not overflow you.
When you walk through the fire, you shall not be
    burned,
Nor shall the flame scorch you.

Isaiah 43:2

Let all those rejoice who put their trust in You;
Let them ever shout for joy, because You defend them;
Let those also who love Your name
Be joyful in You.
For You, O Lord, will bless the righteous;
With favor You will surround him as with a shield.

Psalm 5:11–12

The angel of the Lord encamps all around those who
fear Him, and delivers them.

Psalm 34:7

The horse is prepared for the day of battle,
But deliverance is of the Lord.

Proverbs 21:31

He who dwells in the secret place of the Most High
Shall abide under the shadow of the Almighty.
I will say of the LORD, "He is my refuge and my
fortress;
My God, in Him I will trust."
Surely He shall deliver you from the snare of the fowler
And from the perilous pestilence.
He shall cover you with His feathers,
And under His wings you shall take refuge;
His truth shall be your shield and buckler.
You shall not be afraid of the terror by night,
Nor of the arrow that flies by day,
Nor of the pestilence that walks in darkness,
Nor of the destruction that lays waste at noonday.
A thousand may fall at your side,
And ten thousand at your right hand;
But it shall not come near you.
Only with your eyes shall you look,
And see the reward of the wicked.
Because you have made the LORD, who is my refuge,
Even the Most High, your dwelling place,
No evil shall befall you,
Nor shall any plague come near your dwelling.

PSALM 91:1–10

The fear of man brings a snare,
But whoever trusts in the LORD shall be safe.

PROVERBS 29:25

I will both lie down in peace, and sleep;
For You alone, O LORD, make me dwell in safety.

PSALM 4:8

Yea, though I walk through the valley of the shadow
   of death,
I will fear no evil;
For You are with me;
Your rod and Your staff, they comfort me.

PSALM 23:4

So shall they fear
The name of the LORD from the west,
And His glory from the rising of the sun;
When the enemy comes in like a flood,
The Spirit of the LORD will lift up a standard against
   him.

ISAIAH 59:19

How to Find Contentment

Therefore do not worry, saying, "What shall we eat?" or "What shall we drink?" or "What shall we wear?"

For after all these things the Gentiles seek. For your heavenly Father knows that you need all these things.

But seek first the kingdom of God and His righteousness, and all these things shall be added to you.

Therefore do not worry about tomorrow, for tomorrow will worry about its own things. Sufficient for the day is its own trouble.

MATTHEW 6:31–34

You will keep him in perfect peace,
Whose mind is stayed on You,
Because he trusts in You.
Trust in the LORD forever,
For in YAH, the LORD, is everlasting strength.

ISAIAH 26:3–4

We know that all things work together for good to those who love God, to those who are the called according to His purpose.

ROMANS 8:28

The LORD upholds all who fall,
And raises up all who are bowed down.
The eyes of all look expectantly to You,
And You give them their food in due season.
You open Your hand
And satisfy the desire of every living thing.

PSALM 145:14–16

Let your conduct be without covetousness; be content with such things as you have. For He Himself has said, "I will never leave you nor forsake you."

So we may boldly say: "The LORD is my helper; I will not fear. What can man do to me?"

HEBREWS 13:5–6

He who dwells in the secret place of the Most High
Shall abide under the shadow of the Almighty.
I will say of the LORD, "He is my refuge and my
    fortress;
My God, in Him I will trust."

PSALM 91:1–2

But I discipline my body and bring it into subjection, lest, when I have preached to others, I myself should become disqualified.

1 CORINTHIANS 9:27

Be anxious for nothing, but in everything by prayer and supplication, with thanksgiving, let your requests be made known to God; and the peace of God, which surpasses all understanding, will guard your hearts and minds through Christ Jesus.

Not that I speak in regard to need, for I have learned in whatever state I am, to be content: I know how to be abased, and I know how to abound. Everywhere and in all things I have learned both to be full and to be hungry, both to abound and to suffer need.

I can do all things through Christ who strengthens me.

PHILIPPIANS 4:6, 7, 11–13

Now godliness with contentment is great gain.

For we brought nothing into this world, and it is certain we can carry nothing out.

And having food and clothing, with these we shall be content.

1 TIMOTHY 6:6–8

To be carnally minded is death, but to be spiritually minded is life and peace.

ROMANS 8:6

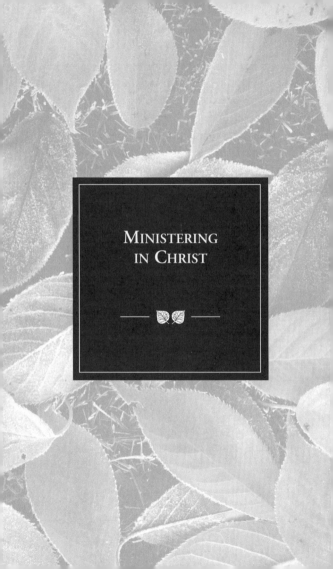

MINISTERING
IN CHRIST

WHAT IS TRUE SERVICE?

When He had called the people to Himself, with His disciples also, He said to them, "Whoever desires to come after Me, let him deny himself, and take up his cross, and follow Me.

"For whoever desires to save his life will lose it, but whoever loses his life for My sake and the gospel's will save it.

"For what will it profit a man if he gains the whole world, and loses his own soul?

"Or what will a man give in exchange for his soul?"

MARK 8:34–37

Abide in Me, and I in you. As the branch cannot bear fruit of itself, unless it abides in the vine, neither can you, unless you abide in Me.

I am the vine, you are the branches. He who abides in Me, and I in him, bears much fruit; for without Me you can do nothing.

JOHN 15:4–5

By this all will know that you are My disciples, if you have love for one another.

JOHN 13:35

For we do not preach ourselves, but Christ Jesus the Lord, and ourselves your bondservants for Jesus' sake.

For it is the God who commanded light to shine out of darkness, who has shone in our hearts to give the light of the knowledge of the glory of God in the face of Jesus Christ.

But we have this treasure in earthen vessels, that the excellence of the power may be of God and not of us.

2 CORINTHIANS 4:5–7

And whatever you do, do it heartily, as to the Lord and not to men, knowing that from the Lord you will receive the reward of the inheritance; for you serve the Lord Christ.

But he who does wrong will be repaid for what he has done, and there is no partiality.

COLOSSIANS 3:23–25

You did not choose Me, but I chose you and appointed you that you should go and bear fruit, and that your fruit should remain, that whatever you ask the Father in My name He may give you.

These things I command you, that you love one another.

JOHN 15:16–17

So the people asked him, saying, "What shall we do then?"

He answered and said to them, "He who has two tunics, let him give to him who has none; and he who has food, let him do likewise."

LUKE 3:10–11

That you may become blameless and harmless, children of God without fault in the midst of a crooked and perverse generation, among whom you shine as lights in the world, holding fast the word of life, so that I may rejoice in the day of Christ that I have not run in vain or labored in vain.

PHILIPPIANS 2:15–16

Command those who are rich in this present age not to be haughty, nor to trust in uncertain riches but in the living God, who gives us richly all things to enjoy.

Let them do good, that they be rich in good works, ready to give, willing to share, storing up for themselves a good foundation for the time to come, that they may lay hold on eternal life.

1 TIMOTHY 6:17–19

He who calls you is faithful, who also will do it.

1 THESSALONIANS 5:24

HOW TO HAVE AN EFFECTIVE PRAYER LIFE

Confess your trespasses to one another, and pray for one another, that you may be healed. The effective, fervent prayer of a righteous man avails much.

Elijah was a man with a nature like ours, and he prayed earnestly that it would not rain; and it did not rain on the land for three years and six months.

And he prayed again, and the heaven gave rain, and the earth produced its fruit.

JAMES 5:16–18

Now in the morning, having risen a long while before daylight, He went out and departed to a solitary place; and there He prayed.

MARK 1:35

Assuredly, I say to you, whatever you bind on earth will be bound in heaven, and whatever you loose on earth will be loosed in heaven.

Again I say to you that if two of you agree on earth concerning anything that they ask, it will be done for them by My Father in heaven.

MATTHEW 18:18–19

LORD, I cry out to You;
Make haste to me!
Give ear to my voice when I cry out to You.
Let my prayer be set before You as incense,
The lifting up of my hands as the evening sacrifice.

PSALM 141:1–2

Be anxious for nothing, but in everything by prayer
and supplication, with thanksgiving, let your requests
be made known to God; and the peace of God, which
surpasses all understanding, will guard your hearts
and minds through Christ Jesus.

PHILIPPIANS 4:6–7

Evening and morning and at noon I will pray, and cry
aloud, and He shall hear my voice.

PSALM 55:17

Without faith it is impossible to please Him, for he
who comes to God must believe that He is, and that
He is a rewarder of those who diligently seek Him.

HEBREWS 11:6

So I say to you, ask, and it will be given to you; seek,
and you will find; knock, and it will be opened to you.

LUKE 11:9

Now it came to pass in those days that He went out to the mountain to pray, and continued all night in prayer to God.

LUKE 6:12

When you pray, you shall not be like the hypocrites. For they love to pray standing in the synagogues and on the corners of the streets, that they may be seen by men. Assuredly, I say to you, they have their reward.

But you, when you pray, go into your room, and when you have shut your door, pray to your Father who is in the secret place; and your Father who sees in secret will reward you openly.

MATTHEW 6:5–6

For the eyes of the LORD are on the righteous,
And His ears are open to their prayers;
But the face of the LORD is against those who do evil.

1 PETER 3:12

So shall My word be that goes forth from My mouth; it shall not return to Me void, but it shall accomplish what I please, and it shall prosper in the thing for which I sent it.

ISAIAH 55:11

HOW TO BE AN EFFECTIVE WITNESS

You are the light of the world. A city that is set on a hill cannot be hidden.

Nor do they light a lamp and put it under a basket, but on a lampstand, and it gives light to all who are in the house.

Let your light so shine before men, that they may see your good works and glorify your Father in heaven.

MATTHEW 5:14–16

No one, when he has lit a lamp, puts it in a secret place or under a basket, but on a lampstand, that those who come in may see the light.

LUKE 11:33

Therefore settle it in your hearts not to meditate beforehand on what you will answer; for I will give you a mouth and wisdom which all your adversaries will not be able to contradict or resist.

LUKE 21:14–15

The fruit of the righteous is a tree of life,
And he who wins souls is wise.

PROVERBS 11:30

Praying always with all prayer and supplication in the Spirit, being watchful to this end with all perseverance and supplication for all the saints—and for me, that utterance may be given to me, that I may open my mouth boldly to make known the mystery of the gospel, for which I am an ambassador in chains; that in it I may speak boldly, as I ought to speak.

EPHESIANS 6:18–20

Therefore do not be ashamed of the testimony of our Lord, nor of me His prisoner, but share with me in the sufferings for the gospel according to the power of God, who has saved us and called us with a holy calling, not according to our works, but according to His own purpose and grace which was given to us in Christ Jesus before time began, but has now been revealed by the appearing of our Savior Jesus Christ, who has abolished death and brought life and immortality to light through the gospel.

2 TIMOTHY 1:8–10

But that the world may know that I love the Father, and as the Father gave Me commandment, so I do. Arise, let us go from here.

JOHN 14:31

Finally, all of you be of one mind, having compassion for one another; love as brothers, be tenderhearted, be courteous; not returning evil for evil or reviling for reviling, but on the contrary blessing, knowing that you were called to this, that you may inherit a blessing.

For "He who would love life and see good days, let him refrain his tongue from evil, and his lips from speaking deceit.

Let him turn away from evil and do good; let him seek peace and pursue it."

But sanctify the Lord God in your hearts, and always be ready to give a defense to everyone who asks you a reason for the hope that is in you, with meekness and fear.

1 PETER 3:8–11, 15

I will sing to the LORD as long as I live;
I will sing praise to my God while I have my being.

PSALM 104:33

Also I say to you, whoever confesses Me before men, him the Son of Man also will confess before the angels of God.

But he who denies Me before men will be denied before the angels of God.

LUKE 12:8–9

How to Handle Condemnation

Blessed are you when men hate you,
And when they exclude you,
And revile you, and cast out your name as evil,
For the Son of Man's sake.
Rejoice in that day and leap for joy!
For indeed your reward is great in heaven,
For in like manner their fathers did to the prophets.

LUKE 6:22–23

If the world hates you, you know that it hated Me before it hated you.

If you were of the world, the world would love its own. Yet because you are not of the world, but I chose you out of the world, therefore the world hates you.

Remember the word that I said to you, "A servant is not greater than his master." If they persecuted Me, they will also persecute you. If they kept My word, they will keep yours also.

But all these things they will do to you for My name's sake, because they do not know Him who sent Me.

JOHN 15:18–21

But even if you should suffer for righteousness' sake, you are blessed. And do not be afraid of their threats, nor be troubled.

But sanctify the Lord God in your hearts, and always be ready to give a defense to everyone who asks you a reason for the hope that is in you, with meekness and fear; having a good conscience, that when they defame you as evildoers, those who revile your good conduct in Christ may be ashamed.

1 PETER 3:14–16

If you are reproached for the name of Christ, blessed are you, for the Spirit of glory and of God rests upon you. On their part He is blasphemed, but on your part He is glorified.

Yet if anyone suffers as a Christian, let him not be ashamed, but let him glorify God in this matter.

1 PETER 4:14, 16

Therefore, having been justified by faith, we have peace with God through our Lord Jesus Christ, through whom also we have access by faith into this grace in which we stand, and rejoice in hope of the glory of God.

ROMANS 5:1–2

The LORD has been my defense,
And my God the rock of my refuge.
He has brought on them their own iniquity,
And shall cut them off in their own wickedness;
The LORD our God shall cut them off.

PSALM 94:22–23

My eyes shall be on the faithful of the land,
That they may dwell with me;
He who walks in a perfect way,
He shall serve me.
He who works deceit shall not dwell within my house;
He who tells lies shall not continue in my presence.

PSALM 101:6–7

Persecutions, afflictions, which happened to me at Antioch, at Iconium, at Lystra—what persecutions I endured. And out of them all the Lord delivered me.

Yes, and all who desire to live godly in Christ Jesus will suffer persecution.

2 TIMOTHY 3:11–12

Do not say, "I will recompense evil";
Wait for the LORD, and He will save you.

PROVERBS 20:22

UNDERSTANDING THE LEADING
OF THE LORD

The LORD will guide you continually,
And satisfy your soul in drought,
And strengthen your bones;
You shall be like a watered garden,
And like a spring of water, whose waters do not fail.

ISAIAH 58:11

I say to you that likewise there will be more joy in heaven over one sinner who repents than over ninety-nine just persons who need no repentance.

LUKE 15:7

"For My thoughts are not your thoughts,
Nor are your ways My ways," says the LORD.
"For as the heavens are higher than the earth,
So are My ways higher than your ways,
And My thoughts than your thoughts."

ISAIAH 55:8–9

The spirit of a man is the lamp of the LORD,
Searching all the inner depths of his heart.

PROVERBS 20:27

The Son of Man has come to save that which was lost.

MATTHEW 18:11

Beloved, do not believe every spirit, but test the spirits, whether they are of God; because many false prophets have gone out into the world.

1 JOHN 4:1

The Lord is not slack concerning His promise, as some count slackness, but is longsuffering toward us, not willing that any should perish but that all should come to repentance.

2 PETER 3:9

He found him in a desert land
And in the wasteland, a howling wilderness;
He encircled him, He instructed him,
He kept him as the apple of His eye.
As an eagle stirs up its nest,
Hovers over its young,
Spreading out its wings, taking them up,
Carrying them on its wings,
So the LORD alone led him,
And there was no foreign god with him.

DEUTERONOMY 32:10–12

So he shepherded them according to the integrity of
  his heart,
And guided them by the skillfulness of his hands.

PSALM 78:72

> You shall not go out with haste,
> Nor go by flight;
> For the LORD will go before you,
> And the God of Israel will be your rear guard.

ISAIAH 52:12

There are three that bear witness in heaven: the Father,
the Word, and the Holy Spirit; and these three are
one.

1 JOHN 5:7

A man's heart plans his way,
But the LORD directs his steps.
The lot is cast into the lap,
But its every decision is from the LORD.

PROVERBS 16:9, 33

God has not given us a spirit of fear, but of power and
of love and of a sound mind.

2 TIMOTHY 1:7

How to Wait on God

Rest in the LORD, and wait patiently for Him;
Do not fret because of him who prospers in his way,
Because of the man who brings wicked schemes to
    pass.
Cease from anger, and forsake wrath;
Do not fret—it only causes harm.
For evildoers shall be cut off;
But those who wait on the LORD,
They shall inherit the earth.

PSALM 37:7–9

I waited patiently for the LORD;
And He inclined to me,
And heard my cry.
He also brought me up out of a horrible pit,
Out of the miry clay,
And set my feet upon a rock,
And established my steps.
He has put a new song in my mouth—
Praise to our God;
Many will see it and fear,
And will trust in the LORD.

PSALM 40:1–3

How to Wait on God

My soul, wait silently for God alone,
For my expectation is from Him.
He only is my rock and my salvation;
He is my defense;
I shall not be moved.

PSALM 62:5–6

Indeed, let no one who waits on You be ashamed;
Let those be ashamed who deal treacherously without
    cause.
Show me Your ways, O LORD;
Teach me Your paths.
Lead me in Your truth and teach me,
For You are the God of my salvation;
On You I wait all the day.
Let integrity and uprightness preserve me,
For I wait for You.

PSALM 25:3–5, 21

Wait on the LORD; be of good courage, and He shall
strengthen your heart; wait, I say, on the LORD!

PSALM 27:14

I will look to the LORD; I will wait for the God of my
salvation; my God will hear me.

MICAH 7:7

God's Answers

Those who wait on the LORD
Shall renew their strength;
They shall mount up with wings like eagles,
They shall run and not be weary,
They shall walk and not faint.

ISAIAH 40:31

The LORD is good to those who wait for Him,
To the soul who seeks Him.
It is good that one should hope and wait quietly
For the salvation of the LORD.

LAMENTATIONS 3:25–26

And it will be said in that day:
"Behold, this is our God;
We have waited for Him, and He will save us.
This is the LORD;
We have waited for Him;
We will be glad and rejoice in His salvation."

ISAIAH 25:9

The LORD will wait, that He may be gracious to you;
and therefore He will be exalted, that He may have
mercy on you. For the LORD is a God of justice;
blessed are all those who wait for Him.

ISAIAH 30:18

The Importance of Obedience

That all the peoples of the earth may know that the LORD is God; there is no other.

Let your heart therefore be loyal to the LORD our God, to walk in His statutes and keep His commandments, as at this day.

1 KINGS 8:60–61

Be doers of the word, and not hearers only, deceiving yourselves.

JAMES 1:22

Now therefore, if you will indeed obey My voice and keep My covenant, then you shall be a special treasure to Me above all people; for all the earth is Mine.

EXODUS 19:5

So Samuel said:
"Has the LORD as great delight in burnt offerings and sacrifices,
As in obeying the voice of the LORD?
Behold, to obey is better than sacrifice,
And to heed than the fat of rams."

1 SAMUEL 15:22

But Peter and the other apostles answered and said: "We ought to obey God rather than men."

ACTS 5:29

I discipline my body and bring it into subjection, lest, when I have preached to others, I myself should become disqualified.

1 CORINTHIANS 9:27

Casting down arguments and every high thing that exalts itself against the knowledge of God, bringing every thought into captivity to the obedience of Christ.

2 CORINTHIANS 10:5

Whoever has no rule over his own spirit
Is like a city broken down, without walls.

PROVERBS 25:28

He who is faithful in what is least is faithful also in much; and he who is unjust in what is least is unjust also in much.

LUKE 16:10

Behold, You desire truth in the inward parts, and in the hidden part You will make me to know wisdom.

PSALM 51:6

Do not be deceived, God is not mocked; for whatever a man sows, that he will also reap.

For he who sows to his flesh will of the flesh reap corruption, but he who sows to the Spirit will of the Spirit reap everlasting life.

GALATIANS 6:7–8

The world is passing away, and the lust of it; but he who does the will of God abides forever.

1 JOHN 2:17

If anyone does not abide in Me, he is cast out as a branch and is withered; and they gather them and throw them into the fire, and they are burned.

If you abide in Me, and My words abide in you, you will ask what you desire, and it shall be done for you.

If you keep My commandments, you will abide in My love, just as I have kept My Father's commandments and abide in His love.

JOHN 15:6–7, 10

> Now the just shall live by faith;
> But if anyone draws back,
> My soul has no pleasure in him.

HEBREWS 10:38

Giving to God's Work

Do not lay up for yourselves treasures on earth, where moth and rust destroy and where thieves break in and steal; but lay up for yourselves treasures in heaven, where neither moth nor rust destroys and where thieves do not break in and steal.

For where your treasure is, there your heart will be also.

MATTHEW 6:19–21

Now Jesus sat opposite the treasury and saw how the people put money into the treasury. And many who were rich put in much.

Then one poor widow came and threw in two mites, which make a quadrans.

So He called His disciples to Himself and said to them, "Assuredly, I say to you that this poor widow has put in more than all those who have given to the treasury; for they all put in out of their abundance, but she out of her poverty put in all that she had, her whole livelihood."

MARK 12:41–44

Give to the LORD the glory due His name; bring an offering, and come into His courts.

PSALM 96:8

But this I say: He who sows sparingly will also reap sparingly, and he who sows bountifully will also reap bountifully.

So let each one give as he purposes in his heart, not grudgingly or of necessity; for God loves a cheerful giver.

2 CORINTHIANS 9:6–7

But woe to you Pharisees! For you tithe mint and rue and all manner of herbs, and pass by justice and the love of God. These you ought to have done, without leaving the others undone.

LUKE 11:42

He who is faithful in what is least is faithful also in much; and he who is unjust in what is least is unjust also in much.

Therefore if you have not been faithful in the unrighteous mammon, who will commit to your trust the true riches?

LUKE 16:10–11

He who has a generous eye will be blessed, for he gives of his bread to the poor.

PROVERBS 22:9

Therefore bear fruits worthy of repentance, and do not think to say to yourselves, "We have Abraham as our father." For I say to you that God is able to raise up children to Abraham from these stones.

MATTHEW 3:8–9

Does he thank that servant because he did the things that were commanded him? I think not.

So likewise you, when you have done all those things which you are commanded, say, "We are unprofitable servants. We have done what was our duty to do."

LUKE 17:9–10

As soon as the commandment was circulated, the children of Israel brought in abundance the firstfruits of grain and wine, oil and honey, and of all the produce of the field; and they brought in abundantly the tithe of everything.

2 CHRONICLES 31:5

HOPING IN CHRIST

HOW TO COMMIT YOUR LIFE
TO CHRIST

That if you confess with your mouth the Lord Jesus and believe in your heart that God has raised Him from the dead, you will be saved.

For with the heart one believes unto righteousness, and with the mouth confession is made unto salvation.

For the Scripture says, "Whoever believes on Him will not be put to shame."

For there is no distinction between Jew and Greek, for the same Lord over all is rich to all who call upon Him.

For "whoever calls on the name of the LORD shall be saved."

ROMANS 10:9–13

The Lord is not slack concerning His promise, as some count slackness, but is longsuffering toward us, not willing that any should perish but that all should come to repentance.

But grow in the grace and knowledge of our Lord and Savior Jesus Christ. To Him be the glory both now and forever. Amen.

2 PETER 3:9, 18

Seek the LORD while He may be found,
Call upon Him while He is near.
Let the wicked forsake his way,
And the unrighteous man his thoughts;
Let him return to the LORD,
And He will have mercy on him;
And to our God,
For He will abundantly pardon.

ISAIAH 55:6–7

All that the Father gives Me will come to Me, and the one who comes to Me I will by no means cast out.

And this is the will of Him who sent Me, that everyone who sees the Son and believes in Him may have everlasting life; and I will raise him up at the last day.

No one can come to Me unless the Father who sent Me draws him; and I will raise him up at the last day.

It is written in the prophets, "And they shall all be taught by God." Therefore everyone who has heard and learned from the Father comes to Me.

Not that anyone has seen the Father, except He who is from God; He has seen the Father.

Most assuredly, I say to you, he who believes in Me has everlasting life.

JOHN 6:37, 40, 44–47

359

Without faith it is impossible to please Him, for he who comes to God must believe that He is, and that He is a rewarder of those who diligently seek Him.

HEBREWS 11:6

Having been set free from sin, and having become slaves of God, you have your fruit to holiness, and the end, everlasting life.

For the wages of sin is death, but the gift of God is eternal life in Christ Jesus our Lord.

ROMANS 6:22–23

Come now, you who say, "Today or tomorrow we will go to such and such a city, spend a year there, buy and sell, and make a profit"; whereas you do not know what will happen tomorrow. For what is your life? It is even a vapor that appears for a little time and then vanishes away.

Instead you ought to say, "If the Lord wills, we shall live and do this or that."

JAMES 4:13–15

Behold, I stand at the door and knock. If anyone hears My voice and opens the door, I will come in to him and dine with him, and he with Me.

REVELATION 3:20

How to Draw Near to God

Draw near to God and He will draw near to you. Cleanse your hands, you sinners; and purify your hearts, you double-minded.

Lament and mourn and weep! Let your laughter be turned to mourning and your joy to gloom.

Humble yourselves in the sight of the Lord, and He will lift you up.

JAMES 4:8–10

I love those who love me, and those who seek me diligently will find me.

PROVERBS 8:17

Seek the LORD and His strength;
Seek His face evermore!
Remember His marvelous works which He has done, His wonders, and the judgments of His mouth.

1 CHRONICLES 16:11–12

In my distress I called upon the LORD, and cried out to my God; He heard my voice from His temple, and my cry came before Him, even to His ears.

PSALM 18:6

Then you will call upon Me and go and pray to Me,
and I will listen to you.

And you will seek Me and find Me, when you
search for Me with all your heart.

JEREMIAH 29:12–13

As the deer pants for the water brooks,
So pants my soul for You, O God.
My soul thirsts for God, for the living God.
When shall I come and appear before God?
Deep calls unto deep at the noise of Your waterfalls;
All Your waves and billows have gone over me.
The Lord will command His lovingkindness in the
daytime,
And in the night His song shall be with me—
A prayer to the God of my life.

PSALM 42:1–2, 7–8

In the day when I cried out, You answered me, and
made me bold with strength in my soul.

PSALM 138:3

The LORD is near to all who call upon Him, to all
who call upon Him in truth.

PSALM 145:18

How to Draw Near to God

HEAR my cry, O God;
Attend to my prayer.
From the end of the earth I will cry to You,
When my heart is overwhelmed;
Lead me to the rock that is higher than I.

PSALM 61:1–2

My soul, wait silently for God alone,
For my expectation is from Him.

PSALM 62:5

All that the Father gives Me will come to Me, and the one who comes to Me I will by no means cast out.

JOHN 6:37

And the Spirit and the bride say, "Come!" And let him who hears say, "Come!" And let him who thirsts come. Whoever desires, let him take the water of life freely.

REVELATION 22:17

How to Recover Spiritually

Have you not known?
Have you not heard?
The everlasting God, the LORD,
The Creator of the ends of the earth,
Neither faints nor is weary.
His understanding is unsearchable.
He gives power to the weak,
And to those who have no might He increases
    strength.
But those who wait on the LORD
Shall renew their strength;
They shall mount up with wings like eagles,
They shall run and not be weary,
They shall walk and not faint.

ISAIAH 40:28–29, 31

For You, Lord, are good, and ready to forgive,
And abundant in mercy to all those who call upon You.
Give ear, O LORD, to my prayer;
And attend to the voice of my supplications.
In the day of my trouble I will call upon You,
For You will answer me.

PSALM 86:5–7

Now no chastening seems to be joyful for the present, but painful; nevertheless, afterward it yields the peaceable fruit of righteousness to those who have been trained by it.

Therefore strengthen the hands which hang down, and the feeble knees, and make straight paths for your feet, so that what is lame may not be dislocated, but rather be healed.

Pursue peace with all people, and holiness, without which no one will see the Lord.

HEBREWS 12:11–14

Blessed is the man whom You instruct, O LORD,
And teach out of Your law,
That You may give him rest from the days of adversity,
Until the pit is dug for the wicked.
For the LORD will not cast off His people,
Nor will He forsake His inheritance.

PSALM 94:12–14

Before I was afflicted I went astray,
But now I keep Your word.
You are good, and do good;
Teach me Your statutes.

PSALM 119:67–68

He who covers his sins will not prosper, but whoever confesses and forsakes them will have mercy.

PROVERBS 28:13

"I will seek what was lost and bring back what was driven away, bind up the broken and strengthen what was sick; but I will destroy the fat and the strong, and feed them in judgment.

"Thus they shall know that I, the LORD their God, am with them, and they, the house of Israel, are My people," says the Lord GOD. "You are My flock, the flock of My pasture; you are men, and I am your God."

EZEKIEL 34:16, 30–31

Poverty and shame will come to him who disdains correction, but he who regards a rebuke will be honored.

PROVERBS 13:18

> When my soul fainted within me,
> I remembered the LORD;
> And my prayer went up to You,
> Into Your holy temple.

JONAH 2:7

How to Obtain God's Promises

By which have been given to us exceedingly great and precious promises, that through these you may be partakers of the divine nature, having escaped the corruption that is in the world through lust.

But also for this very reason, giving all diligence, add to your faith virtue, to virtue knowledge, to knowledge self-control, to self-control perseverance, to perseverance godliness, to godliness brotherly kindness, and to brotherly kindness love.

For if these things are yours and abound, you will be neither barren nor unfruitful in the knowledge of our Lord Jesus Christ.

2 PETER 1:4–8

Let us hold fast the confession of our hope without wavering, for He who promised is faithful.

Therefore do not cast away your confidence, which has great reward.

For you have need of endurance, so that after you have done the will of God, you may receive the promise: "For yet a little while, and He who is coming will come and will not tarry."

HEBREWS 10:23, 35–37

If you carefully keep all these commandments which I command you to do—to love the LORD your God, to walk in all His ways, and to hold fast to Him— then the LORD will drive out all these nations from before you, and you will dispossess greater and mightier nations than yourselves.

DEUTERONOMY 11:22–23

Only be strong and very courageous, that you may observe to do according to all the law which Moses My servant commanded you; do not turn from it to the right hand or to the left, that you may prosper wherever you go.

JOSHUA 1:7

For assuredly, I say to you, whoever says to this mountain, "Be removed and be cast into the sea," and does not doubt in his heart, but believes that those things he says will be done, he will have whatever he says.

MARK 11:23

Do not become sluggish, but imitate those who through faith and patience inherit the promises.

HEBREWS 6:12

Now faith is the substance of things hoped for, the evidence of things not seen.

But without faith it is impossible to please Him, for he who comes to God must believe that He is, and that He is a rewarder of those who diligently seek Him.

By faith Sarah herself also received strength to conceive seed, and she bore a child when she was past the age, because she judged Him faithful who had promised.

HEBREWS 11:1, 6, 11

Now this is the confidence that we have in Him, that if we ask anything according to His will, He hears us.

And if we know that He hears us, whatever we ask, we know that we have the petitions that we have asked of Him.

1 JOHN 5:14–15

If you are willing and obedient,
You shall eat the good of the land;
But if you refuse and rebel,
You shall be devoured by the sword;
For the mouth of the LORD has spoken.

ISAIAH 1:19–20

If any of you lacks wisdom, let him ask of God, who gives to all liberally and without reproach, and it will be given to him.

But let him ask in faith, with no doubting, for he who doubts is like a wave of the sea driven and tossed by the wind.

For let not that man suppose that he will receive anything from the Lord; he is a double-minded man, unstable in all his ways.

JAMES 1:5–8

For with God nothing will be impossible.

LUKE 1:37

Behold, the LORD's hand is not shortened,
That it cannot save;
Nor His ear heavy,
That it cannot hear.
But your iniquities have separated you from your God;
And your sins have hidden His face from you,
So that He will not hear.

ISAIAH 59:1–2

But seek first the kingdom of God and His righteousness, and all these things shall be added to you.

MATTHEW 6:33

UNDERSTANDING
IN CHRIST

Though the LORD is on high,
Yet He regards the lowly;
But the proud He knows from afar.
Though I walk in the midst of trouble, You will revive
   me;
You will stretch out Your hand
Against the wrath of my enemies,
And Your right hand will save me.

PSALM 138:6–7

"For My thoughts are not your thoughts,
  Nor are your ways My ways," says the LORD.
"For as the heavens are higher than the earth,
  So are My ways higher than your ways,
  And My thoughts than your thoughts."

ISAIAH 55:8–9

As a father pities his children,
So the LORD pities those who fear Him.
For He knows our frame;
He remembers that we are dust.

PSALM 103:13–14

As for God, His way is perfect;
The word of the LORD is proven;
He is a shield to all who trust in Him.
For who is God, except the LORD?
And who is a rock, except our God?
It is God who arms me with strength,
And makes my way perfect.

PSALM 18:30–32

I, the LORD, search the heart,
I test the mind,
Even to give every man according to his ways,
According to the fruit of his doings.

JEREMIAH 17:10

Jesus said to them, "Have you never read in the
Scriptures:
'The stone which the builders rejected
Has become the chief cornerstone.
This was the LORD's doing,
And it is marvelous in our eyes'?"

MATTHEW 21:42

373

Every good gift and every perfect gift is from above, and comes down from the Father of lights, with whom there is no variation or shadow of turning.

JAMES 1:17

He has made the earth by His power,
He has established the world by His wisdom,
And has stretched out the heavens at His discretion.

JEREMIAH 10:12

The LORD is in His holy temple,
The LORD's throne is in heaven;
His eyes behold,
His eyelids test the sons of men.
The LORD tests the righteous,
But the wicked and the one who loves violence His
    soul hates.
For the LORD is righteous,
He loves righteousness;
His countenance beholds the upright.

PSALM 11:4–5, 7

Now therefore, let the fear of the Lord be upon you; take care and do it, for there is no iniquity with the Lord our God, no partiality, nor taking of bribes.

2 CHRONICLES 19:7

How to Receive Understanding

The fear of the LORD is the beginning of wisdom; a good understanding have all those who do His commandments. His praise endures forever.

PSALM 111:10

If any of you lacks wisdom, let him ask of God, who gives to all liberally and without reproach, and it will be given to him.

JAMES 1:5

Counsel is mine, and sound wisdom;
I am understanding, I have strength.

PROVERBS 8:14

Forsake foolishness and live, and go in the way of understanding. "The fear of the LORD is the beginning of wisdom, and the knowledge of the Holy One is understanding."

PROVERBS 9:6, 10

But there is a spirit in man, and the breath of the Almighty gives him understanding.

JOB 32:8

How much better to get wisdom than gold! And to get understanding is to be chosen rather than silver. The highway of the upright is to depart from evil; he who keeps his way preserves his soul.

PROVERBS 16:16–17

Understanding is a wellspring of life to him who has it. But the correction of fools is folly.

PROVERBS 16:22

Incline your ear, and come to Me.
Hear, and your soul shall live;
And I will make an everlasting covenant with you—
The sure mercies of David.
Seek the LORD while He may be found,
Call upon Him while He is near.
"For My thoughts are not your thoughts,
Nor are your ways My ways," says the LORD.
"For as the heavens are higher than the earth,
So are My ways higher than your ways,
And My thoughts than your thoughts."

ISAIAH 55:3, 6, 8–9

How to Receive Understanding

Yes, if you cry out for discernment,
And lift up your voice for understanding,
If you seek her as silver,
And search for her as for hidden treasures;
Then you will understand the fear of the LORD,
And find the knowledge of God.
For the LORD gives wisdom;
From His mouth come knowledge and understanding;
He stores up sound wisdom for the upright;
He is a shield to those who walk uprightly;
He guards the paths of justice,
And preserves the way of His saints.
Then you will understand righteousness and justice,
Equity and every good path.
When wisdom enters your heart,
And knowledge is pleasant to your soul,
Discretion will preserve you;
Understanding will keep you.

PROVERBS 2:3–11

Understanding the Fear of the Lord

In the fear of the LORD there is strong confidence,
And His children will have a place of refuge.
The fear of the LORD is a fountain of life,
To turn one away from the snares of death.

PROVERBS 14:26–27

He does not delight in the strength of the horse;
He takes no pleasure in the legs of a man.
The LORD takes pleasure in those who fear Him,
In those who hope in His mercy.

PSALM 147:10–11

If you seek her as silver,
And search for her as for hidden treasures;
Then you will understand the fear of the LORD,
And find the knowledge of God.

PROVERBS 2:4–5

The fear of the LORD is the beginning of wisdom,
And the knowledge of the Holy One is understanding.

PROVERBS 9:10

The fear of the LORD is the instruction of wisdom, and before honor is humility.

PROVERBS 15:33

The fear of the LORD is the beginning of knowledge, but fools despise wisdom and instruction.

PROVERBS 1:7

The fear of the LORD leads to life, and he who has it will abide in satisfaction; he will not be visited with evil.

PROVERBS 19:23

And to man He said, "Behold, the fear of the Lord, that is wisdom, and to depart from evil is understanding."

JOB 28:28

The fear of the LORD prolongs days, but the years of the wicked will be shortened.

PROVERBS 10:27

Oh, fear the LORD, you His saints! There is no want to those who fear Him.

PSALM 34:9

The LORD is righteous in all His ways,
Gracious in all His works.
The LORD is near to all who call upon Him,
To all who call upon Him in truth.
He will fulfill the desire of those who fear Him;
He also will hear their cry and save them.

PSALM 145:17–19

Praise the LORD!
Blessed is the man who fears the LORD,
Who delights greatly in His commandments.

PSALM 112:1

Let us hear the conclusion of the whole matter:
Fear God and keep His commandments,
For this is man's all.
For God will bring every work into judgment,
Including every secret thing,
Whether good or evil.

ECCLESIASTES 12:13–14

UNDERSTANDING THE SOVEREIGNTY OF GOD

The LORD is our Judge, the LORD is our Lawgiver, the LORD is our King; He will save us.

ISAIAH 33:22

"Am I a God near at hand," says the LORD,
"And not a God afar off?
  Can anyone hide himself in secret places,
  So I shall not see him?" says the LORD;
"Do I not fill heaven and earth?" says the LORD.

JEREMIAH 23:23–24

Where were you when I laid the foundations of the
    earth?
Tell Me, if you have understanding.
Who determined its measurements?
Surely you know!
Or who stretched the line upon it?
To what were its foundations fastened?
Or who laid its cornerstone,
When the morning stars sang together,
And all the sons of God shouted for joy?

JOB 38:4–7

All nations before Him are as nothing,
And they are counted by Him less than nothing and
   worthless.
To whom then will you liken God?
Or what likeness will you compare to Him?
"To whom then will you liken Me,
Or to whom shall I be equal?" says the Holy One.
Lift up your eyes on high,
And see who has created these things,
Who brings out their host by number;
He calls them all by name,
By the greatness of His might
And the strength of His power;
Not one is missing.
Have you not known?
Have you not heard?
The everlasting God, the LORD,
The Creator of the ends of the earth,
Neither faints nor is weary.
His understanding is unsearchable.

ISAIAH 40:17, 18, 25, 26, 28

Behold, I am the LORD, the God of all flesh. Is there
anything too hard for Me?

JEREMIAH 32:27

Thus says the LORD:
"Heaven is My throne,
And earth is My footstool.
Where is the house that you will build Me?
And where is the place of My rest?
For all those things My hand has made,
And all those things exist,"
Says the LORD.
"But on this one will I look:
On him who is poor and of a contrite spirit,
And who trembles at My word."

ISAIAH 66:1–2

Great is the LORD, and greatly to be praised;
And His greatness is unsearchable.
One generation shall praise Your works to another,
And shall declare Your mighty acts.
Your kingdom is an everlasting kingdom,
And Your dominion endures throughout all
generations.

PSALM 145:3–4, 13

The heavens declare the glory of God;
And the firmament shows His handiwork.

PSALM 19:1

And I heard a loud voice from heaven saying, "Behold, the tabernacle of God is with men, and He will dwell with them, and they shall be His people. God Himself will be with them and be their God.

"And God will wipe away every tear from their eyes; there shall be no more death, nor sorrow, nor crying. There shall be no more pain, for the former things have passed away."

Then He who sat on the throne said, "Behold, I make all things new." And He said to me, "Write, for these words are true and faithful."

And He said to me, "It is done! I am the Alpha and the Omega, the Beginning and the End. I will give of the fountain of the water of life freely to him who thirsts."

REVELATION 21:3–6

Those who are wise shall shine
Like the brightness of the firmament,
And those who turn many to righteousness
Like the stars forever and ever.

DANIEL 12:3

For now we see in a mirror, dimly, but then face to face. Now I know in part, but then I shall know just as I also am known.

1 CORINTHIANS 13:12

Assuredly, I say to you, I will no longer drink of the fruit of the vine until that day when I drink it new in the kingdom of God.

MARK 14:25

But as it is written: "Eye has not seen, nor ear heard, nor have entered into the heart of man the things which God has prepared for those who love Him."

But God has revealed them to us through His Spirit. For the Spirit searches all things, yes, the deep things of God.

For what man knows the things of a man except the spirit of the man which is in him? Even so no one knows the things of God except the Spirit of God.

1 CORINTHIANS 2:9–11

For since the beginning of the world
Men have not heard nor perceived by the ear,
Nor has the eye seen any God besides You,
Who acts for the one who waits for Him.

ISAIAH 64:4

God's Answers

Violence shall no longer be heard in your land,
Neither wasting nor destruction within your borders;
But you shall call your walls Salvation,
And your gates Praise.
The sun shall no longer be your light by day,
Nor for brightness shall the moon give light to you;
But the LORD will be to you an everlasting light,
And your God your glory.
Your sun shall no longer go down,
Nor shall your moon withdraw itself;
For the LORD will be your everlasting light,
And the days of your mourning shall be ended.

ISAIAH 60:18–20

Surely goodness and mercy shall follow me all the
     days of my life;
And I will dwell in the house of the LORD forever.

PSALM 23:6

And when I saw Him, I fell at His feet as dead. But
He laid His right hand on me, saying to me, "Do not
be afraid; I am the First and the Last.

"I am He who lives, and was dead, and behold, I
am alive forevermore. Amen. And I have the keys of
Hades and of Death."

REVELATION 1:17–18

UNITING IN CHRIST

You call me Teacher and Lord, and you say well, for so I am.

If I then, your Lord and Teacher, have washed your feet, you also ought to wash one another's feet.

For I have given you an example, that you should do as I have done to you.

Most assuredly, I say to you, a servant is not greater than his master; nor is he who is sent greater than he who sent him.

If you know these things, blessed are you if you do them.

JOHN 13:13–17

Now, therefore, you are no longer strangers and foreigners, but fellow citizens with the saints and members of the household of God, having been built on the foundation of the apostles and prophets, Jesus Christ Himself being the chief cornerstone, in whom the whole building, being fitted together, grows into a holy temple in the Lord, in whom you also are being built together for a dwelling place of God in the Spirit.

EPHESIANS 2:19–22

But now God has set the members, each one of them, in the body just as He pleased.

And if they were all one member, where would the body be?

But now indeed there are many members, yet one body.

And the eye cannot say to the hand, "I have no need of you"; nor again the head to the feet, "I have no need of you."

No, much rather, those members of the body which seem to be weaker are necessary.

And those members of the body which we think to be less honorable, on these we bestow greater honor; and our unpresentable parts have greater modesty, but our presentable parts have no need. But God composed the body, having given greater honor to that part which lacks it, that there should be no schism in the body, but that the members should have the same care for one another.

And if one member suffers, all the members suffer with it; or if one member is honored, all the members rejoice with it.

Now you are the body of Christ, and members individually.

1 CORINTHIANS 12:18–27

Finally, all of you be of one mind, having compassion for one another; love as brothers, be tenderhearted, be courteous; not returning evil for evil or reviling for reviling, but on the contrary blessing, knowing that you were called to this, that you may inherit a blessing.

1 PETER 3:8–9

For you are still carnal. For where there are envy, strife, and divisions among you, are you not carnal and behaving like mere men?

For when one says, "I am of Paul," and another, "I am of Apollos," are you not carnal?

Who then is Paul, and who is Apollos, but ministers through whom you believed, as the Lord gave to each one?

I planted, Apollos watered, but God gave the increase.

So then neither he who plants is anything, nor he who waters, but God who gives the increase.

Now he who plants and he who waters are one, and each one will receive his own reward according to his own labor.

For we are God's fellow workers; you are God's field, you are God's building.

1 CORINTHIANS 3:3–9

THE HOPE FOR REVIVAL

The Lord is not slack concerning His promise, as some count slackness, but is longsuffering toward us, not willing that any should perish but that all should come to repentance.

2 PETER 3:9

Arise, shine;
For your light has come!
And the glory of the LORD is risen upon you.
For behold, the darkness shall cover the earth,
And deep darkness the people;
But the LORD will arise over you,
And His glory will be seen upon you.

ISAIAH 60:1–2

This gospel of the kingdom will be preached in all the world as a witness to all the nations, and then the end will come.

MATTHEW 24:14

The earth will be filled with the knowledge of the glory of the LORD, as the waters cover the sea.

HABAKKUK 2:14

And they shall rebuild the old ruins,
They shall raise up the former desolations,
And they shall repair the ruined cities,
The desolations of many generations.
For as the earth brings forth its bud,
As the garden causes the things that are sown in it to
    spring forth,
So the Lord GOD will cause righteousness and praise
    to spring forth before all the nations.

ISAIAH 61:4, 11

All the ends of the world
Shall remember and turn to the LORD,
And all the families of the nations
Shall worship before You.
For the kingdom is the LORD's,
And He rules over the nations.

PSALM 22:27–28

Therefore be patient, brethren, until the coming of
the Lord. See how the farmer waits for the precious
fruit of the earth, waiting patiently for it until it
receives the early and latter rain.

JAMES 5:7

The Hope for Revival

And it shall come to pass afterward
That I will pour out My Spirit on all flesh;
Your sons and your daughters shall prophesy,
Your old men shall dream dreams,
Your young men shall see visions.
And also on My menservants and on My maidservants
I will pour out My Spirit in those days.
And I will show wonders in the heavens and in the
  earth:
Blood and fire and pillars of smoke.
The sun shall be turned into darkness,
And the moon into blood,
Before the coming of the great and awesome day of
  the LORD.
And it shall come to pass
That whoever calls on the name of the LORD
Shall be saved.
For in Mount Zion and in Jerusalem there shall be
  deliverance,
As the LORD has said,
Among the remnant whom the LORD calls.

JOEL 2:28–32

Then two men will be in the field: one will be taken and the other left.

Watch therefore, for you do not know what hour your Lord is coming.

Therefore you also be ready, for the Son of Man is coming at an hour you do not expect.

MATTHEW 24:40, 42, 44

But know this, that in the last days perilous times will come: For men will be lovers of themselves, lovers of money, boasters, proud, blasphemers, disobedient to parents, unthankful, unholy, unloving, unforgiving, slanderers, without self-control, brutal, despisers of good, traitors, headstrong, haughty, lovers of pleasure rather than lovers of God, having a form of godliness but denying its power. And from such people turn away!

2 TIMOTHY 3:1–5

Christ was offered once to bear the sins of many. To those who eagerly wait for Him He will appear a second time, apart from sin, for salvation.

HEBREWS 9:28

And Jesus answered and said to them: "Take heed that no one deceives you.

"For many will come in My name, saying, 'I am the Christ,' and will deceive many.

"And you will hear of wars and rumors of wars. See that you are not troubled; for all these things must come to pass, but the end is not yet.

"For nation will rise against nation, and kingdom against kingdom. And there will be famines, pestilences, and earthquakes in various places.

"All these are the beginning of sorrows.

"Then they will deliver you up to tribulation and kill you, and you will be hated by all nations for My name's sake.

"And then many will be offended, will betray one another, and will hate one another.

"Then many false prophets will rise up and deceive many.

"And because lawlessness will abound, the love of many will grow cold.

"But he who endures to the end shall be saved.

"And this gospel of the kingdom will be preached in all the world as a witness to all the nations, and then the end will come."

MATTHEW 24:4–14

Now the Spirit expressly says that in latter times some will depart from the faith, giving heed to deceiving spirits and doctrines of demons, speaking lies in hypocrisy, having their own conscience seared with a hot iron, forbidding to marry, and commanding to abstain from foods which God created to be received with thanksgiving by those who believe and know the truth.

1 TIMOTHY 4:1–3

But you, beloved, remember the words which were spoken before by the apostles of our Lord Jesus Christ: how they told you that there would be mockers in the last time who would walk according to their own ungodly lusts.

These are sensual persons, who cause divisions, not having the Spirit.

But you, beloved, building yourselves up on your most holy faith, praying in the Holy Spirit, keep yourselves in the love of God, looking for the mercy of our Lord Jesus Christ unto eternal life.

JUDE 17–21